A Plain Brown Wren

This is a true story, but the names and other identifying characteristics of certain persons depicted in this book have been changed in order to protect their privacy. The events portrayed in this book are accurate to the best of the author's recollection.

ISBN: 1-4196-3223-X
ISBN-13: 978-1419632235
Library of Congress Control Number: 2006902263

Visit www.booksurge.com to order additional copies.

HILDA THOMASINE
WREN

A PLAIN BROWN WREN

2007

A Plain Brown Wren

DYNAMICS OF BLACK SEXUAL ABUSE

I have often suggested in the thirty-nine years of my practice in General Psychiatry and Child Psychiatry, that a patient should one day write about their life experiences, as yet another means of mastering the experiences—especially those that have been painful.

The personal memoir, *A Plain Brown Wren*, by Hilda Thomasine Wren represents just such an important endeavor. Hers is a spiritual odyssey, in many ways a sermon of success, that must be placed in its full context if in fact it is to be fully understood.

Just as one small piece of a large puzzle, no matter how complete its small image, it is not fully understood until the entire puzzle has been assembled.

The total dynamic context in which I place the experiences of Hilda Thomasine Wren, is inclusive of the multiple centuries (non-stop) of the enslavement of African peoples in the Americas and Caribbean. Although seldom spoken of as such, it was much more than the dehumanization of the middle passage, chains and unpaid labor. It was inclusive of continuous daily sexual abuse and assault, continuous physical abuse and assault and the daily psychological abuse of men, women and children.

The chains of the formal enslavement of Black people may have been removed in the mid 19th century, but that ended only one phase of the entire system of Racism (White Supremacy) which has continued to the present by other means, in all areas of life activity (economics, education, entertainment, labor, law, politics, religion, sex and war)—to achieve the same end of Black oppression.

The tsunami size shock waves and the after-shocks of the continuous sexual and psychological abuses begun by White Slave masters and White slave mistresses, crashing against the lives of the individual enslaved African peoples, continues after tens of generations, to crash ashore in the present—in the individual lives of Black people. This is so because the powerful dynamic substrate of Racism (White Supremacy) remains. It surrounds and engulfs the lives of all Black people, echoing the message,

"You are nothing—and it means nothing, if you are demeaned and abused."

But the spiritual journey of Hilda Thomasine Wren and the courageous effort she has made towards her own self-recovery and self-mastery, in documenting her very personal experience, is a reflection of the powerful human energy and resolve that will one day bring to an end, any and all attempts to demean and degrade the human beings on planet Earth.

The flight of *A Plain Brown Wren* is showing the way.

I wish for her a continuing God Speed.

Frances Cress Welsing, MD
February 19, 2007

ACKNOWLEDGEMENTS

I would like to personally thank all of my medical doctors and alternative practitioners: Dr. Frances Cress Welsing, my psychiatrist; Michael H. Gillooly, my therapist; Dr. Catherine Brophy, my primary care physician; and Mrs. Terry L. Tipton, president of the Terry Tipton Foundation at Far Cry Farms Holistic Retreat, my first medical intuitive/energy practitioner.

For their assistance and support, I thank Wallace Lossing and Beverly Sweetman, Euric Herman, Shellie Lambert, Robin Montgomery, Nancy Hickman, Tony Farmer, and Suzanne Pierce.

For my spiritual growth and counsel, I thank my pastor, Rev. Jim Webb, senior pastor of The Takoma Park Chapel, and my mentor and friend Rev. Dr. Alice V. Thompson. I am forever grateful to my family who supported me through this whole process; Jenetha McCutcheon, my sister in a past life and my editor; Rev. Dr. Tunde Adenuga, my other mentor and classmate; and all others I have not named.

A personal thank you goes to the board of directors for Spiritual Connections, Inc., a foundation created to help women and children heal from childhood sexual abuse. I do not know what I would have done without them.

For all of you who were "there" for me, I give you my undying love and gratitude.

I Dedicate This Book To James And Mazie Booze And Esther V. Hamilton. I Truly Believe That Their Spirits Walk With Me Every Day. I Love All Of Them Even More Now Than When They Were Alive. I Would Like To Also Dedicate This Book To All Those Who Have Suffered Any Kind Of Sexual, Physical Or Emotional Abuse. I Often Think About The Children In Africa Who Still Suffer From Many Different Forms Of Abuse. It Is Very Painful And Humiliating For The Victims And Has Lifelong Ramifications.

FOREWORD

My name is Michael H. Gillooly and I have been one of Thomasine's therapists on her journey of healing and discovery since 2002. I am a licensed professional social worker, personal coach, and advanced Eye Movement Desensitization & Reprocessing (EMDR) practitioner with 23 years experience helping children, adolescents, couples, families, and individuals. I specialize in Trauma (Post Traumatic Stress Disorder (PTSD)) Treatment/Recovery; Child/Adolescent Counseling; Holistic Migraine and Tension Headache Relief; Stress Management; Father/Parent-Child Coaching; School Performance & Behavior Modification; and Adoptive and Step Parent Counseling. I am an LCSW-C, which means I am a Licensed Clinical Social Worker in the State of Maryland. I have been in practice as a psychotherapist since 1983, starting my career working on a trauma hotline. I have worked as a child protective services professional, as a family therapist at a mental health clinic on a children's team for 11 years, the last six of which were as Director of the children's team, and in full-time private practice since 1997.

When I first met Thomasine Wren she had an obvious diagnosis of post traumatic stress disorder. She began to address her long history of trauma after she experienced what she calls her "nervous breakdown" while working for the federal government. In reality, this was the final straw that put her over the edge. Prior to this event, Thomasine had already experienced one of the most extensive histories of traumas as a child and as an adult of any client I have ever worked with. That she was still a functioning adult in the federal government is part of what is so amazing about the strength of Thomasine. While she has struggled with her anger at times, she is generally a kind, generous person; sometimes too generous.

In 2002, when Thomasine came to see me, she knew she was looking to take the next step in her journey but was not sure what this step looked like. Together we figured it out. What has always been impressive about Thomasine is her willingness to try various alternative methods of healing. She does not do this in a reckless, careless manner but from a willingness to do whatever it takes her to heal and move on. Part of what I was able to offer her included energy therapies such as EMDR, a treatment invented by Dr. Francine Shapiro, and Emotional Freedom Techniques (EFT) a less complicated version of Thought Field Therapy (TFT) invented by Dennis Callahan. EMDR involves bilateral stimulation of the brain and focuses on the kinesthetic, auditory, and visual senses involved in experiencing and storing all traumas. I began using this therapy after being trained by Dr. Shapiro in 1993. EMDR is now a scientifically proven approach to treating PTSD as demonstrated in over 20 clinical studies. It is widely used by the U.S. Department of Veterans Affairs and Department of Defense, the United Kingdom Department of Health, the Israeli National Council for Mental Health, and many other international health and governmental agencies. Research has shown that EMDR is an efficient and rapid treatment modality of PTSD symptoms. I have used it with adults as well as children for almost 14 years, providing relief to clients suffering from a broad range of issues and associated symptoms, not just PTSD. EFT involves tapping various acupuncture pressure points along with various statements such as "even though I'm very upset about (issue), I truly and deeply accept myself." This is what Thomasine refers to as tapping therapy. Both of these very effective techniques are used to treat negative energy issues such as PTSD, anxiety, anger, stress, headaches, and so on, as well as positive energy work that helps individuals and even couples explore and experience growth in their personal and professional lives.

Healing from repetitive instances of trauma and the corresponding therapeutic path individuals take to get there is an evolutionary and iterative process. I feel privileged to be a part of Thomasine's journey. Thomasine has written her story a number of times, and as she grew so did the strength of her story. This evolution reflects her progress and personal growth in dealing with the traumas she experienced and ultimately the health and happiness she has found. It is a story of hope. She has gone from a time when she felt overwhelmed by the flashbacks of these traumas to a place of strength where she is able to offer help to others affected by childhood trauma through her work as a minister and her volunteer efforts at a hospital supporting rape victims. This book is just one example of her efforts to reach out to other victims of childhood trauma and share the journey she is still taking. She still has her struggles yet remains committed to her healing.

This book is engrossing because of Thomasine's honesty and the story itself. She demonstrates that healing is possible even with a history like hers. Her message has always been, "If someone knows my story, maybe it will give them hope that they too can heal." As a therapist, I know from over 20 years experience that healing comes in many forms, sometimes quickly, sometimes more slowly, using a variety of different techniques. I encourage everyone who has experienced trauma or just needs a helping hand to reach out and claim the support you need to heal and move on to a happier, healthier life. As Thomasine's message shows, it really can be done.

INTRODUCTION

Just think, on September 1, 2005, I was preparing for graduation from the All Faith Seminary International as an Interfaith Minister. I became a minister as a result of my own healing journey. This allows me to share my faith and experience with others with hopes of inspiring them to begin healing from sexual, emotional or physical abuse.

Before I begin my story, I want to share with you my belief that we all view and plan the events of our lives, and create our astrological life charts, before being born. We make agreements with our parents, siblings, children and friends. We enter into a spiritual agreement with God to come here to experience joy, healing, pain, suffering, and other emotions, and to learn our lessons through the people we chose to experience life with. I believe in the concept of reincarnation and that we live and die over and over again until we learn all we need to know. In my case, I believe I have learned most of my spiritual lessons this time around and I learned them with intensity.

My life has been an uphill battle from day one but I am a strong person and Mother/Father God has been with me every step of the way. Today I can say I wouldn't change any of my experiences.

I initially wrote my story as a way to heal. Now, I want to tell it to help others in their healing process, therefore; I ask you to read this book as a tool for your own healing journey. I am a survivor and no longer a victim in this life. I thank Mother/Father God for giving me the opportunity to serve others. I also thank Mother/Father God for keeping me here to write this book because there were many times when my self-destructive behavior could have ended my life. There were many times when I wanted to die. But I didn't. I chose to utilize therapy, alternative health practitioners, self-help books, and tapes. Those things helped me find my true path in life and to be more loving in the choices I make for myself. This book describes my journey of healing and awakening to my path of helping other victims of abuse.

While I do not promote profanity, this book was written as a journal and contains profanity and graphic scenes that represent where I was in my healing journey. It expresses the deepest emotions I experienced as a result of the trauma of abuse, and I would like it to be an example of the depths of pain abuse can cause. The journaling of this book was the greatest healing for me. As you read it, please know that I was a child when most of the abuse occurred. Also, I am no longer the person of my past, and I do not condone living an unhealthy lifestyle.

The process I used to heal was what worked for me. I do not expect you, the reader, to do everything I did. We all have free will and the readers should choose the path most comfortable for themselves. Just recognize that you have options for healing that you may not have explored. When you get tired of the vicious cycle of abuse, you can change the painful patterns of your life. Healing is possible.

CHAPTER 1
History of My Family

I've been told that I came here as a very old soul and I believe that to be true. I was born to two individuals who were very immature and had a lot of issues. My mother and my biological father were married in 1943. He was 29 and she was 31 when I was born. I was told that my father hated his own father because he blamed him for his mother's mental breakdown. He believed that his mother had all three of her children too close and that caused her to have a mental decline. I was told that she died in an institution soon after my father was born.

My father's father remarried after his first wife died. His new wife didn't want the responsibility of raising three little children, so in order to keep her happy, my grandfather sent my father and his two sisters, Della and Etta, to an orphanage in Staunton, Virginia. They remained in the orphanage during the winter months and spent their summers with their parents in Charlottesville, Virginia.

My mother had two loving parents who worked hard on a big farm and raised nine children. My mother, the oldest child, and her siblings were born and raised in Sunderland, Maryland. At last count, I have 35 first cousins and over 37 second cousins.

My mother had a son, Phillip Christopher Horner, out of wedlock at age 17. Her mother convinced her to marry a man from the Sunderland area who was not Phillip's father, right after his birth. That marriage only lasted seven months. After it ended, my mother took a job in Washington, D.C. to support Phillip who was being raised by his maternal grandparents.

My mother and biological father met in Washington, D.C., and they got married in 1943 at John Wesley AME Zion Methodist Church. He promised her that once they were married he would have Phillip move in with them, because he truly wanted a son. Phillip came to visit for two weeks during their first summer together, but before the two weeks ended, he told her that Phillip would have to go back to his grandparents.

In his words, he felt "as if another man was living in the house" with them. That betrayal by my father angered my mother, and she made a promise to herself that she would not share any children with him.

I was born 11:21 a.m. on November 21, 1950 at Garfield's Hospital in Washington, D.C. I was born with weak eye muscles, which caused me to have crossed eyes. In addition to the abuse I suffered later in childhood, my eye problem has been a constant emotional struggle for me my whole life.

Just prior to my conception, my parents were having problems in their marriage. My mother told me that my biological father had come home one night frustrated about their relationship and announced that he was in love with someone else. Apparently, they were trying to work on the relationship when I was conceived.

Sometime right after I was conceived, my mother met and fell in love with Mr. Matthew Stevens, Sr., who had been injured in the Korean War and was recovering from his wounds at the Bethesda Naval Hospital outside of Washington, D.C. She met Matthew when a friend of my father, Warren Watson, asked him if he would be so kind as to drive him to the hospital to visit Matthew. My father asked her if she wanted to come along for the ride. She did and soon after that visit she and Matthew started dating, fell in love and married. The year was 1955.

Unfortunately, each of the two men was given the impression that I was his child. My mother told the courts that I was not my father's child so that she could get a quick divorce and not have to share me with him. She lied and told Matthew Stevens that I was really his child because she loved him and wanted him to think I was his. DNA testing was not an option for them at that time.

Matthew was a handsome man from Raleigh, North Carolina. Like my biological father, he came from a dysfunctional family. His aunt and uncle raised him and his sister Claire. He was a heavy drinker and had lots of girlfriends, but my mother won his heart.

CHAPTER 2
The Start of My Journey

In 1953, at age three, I had my first eye surgery to correct the weak muscles. The surgery took place at the Episcopal Ear, Eye, Nose and Throat Hospital. I remember fighting my mother all the way across the street because I didn't want to go. I kicked, screamed and wriggled my little body every which way I could to get away from her. She did not let my hand go. I also remember being put to sleep with someone putting a black mask over my face and the awful smelling ether going up my nostrils. I fought until the drug took effect. When I woke up, I was holding my mother's hand. I begged her to take me home, but she would wait for me to fall asleep and then leave. I also remember the nurses tying my hands to the rails of the bed because I pulled the bandages from my eyes. The nurses were quite rough with me. I cried the whole time I was in the hospital.

In December 1954, we moved from the projects on 5th and I Streets, S.E. in Washington, D.C., to a beautiful four bedroom detached brick house in a nearby area. It was perceived at the time that all of the white people who had lived in that area of D.C. had moved to the suburbs of Maryland to get away from us black people.

On May 4, 1955, my brother was born. Matthew was so proud of his son that he placed him in a bassinet in the middle of the living room of the house so everyone could see him. We had a parade of people visiting to see the new baby boy they named Matthew Andre Stevens. I felt unconditional love for my brother the moment I saw him for the first time and my feelings for him have never changed.

My mother had a job making bullets at the Navy Yard when she met a group of women around her age. These ladies were married to men who believed in partying every Friday night just like Matthew. Most of them started partying on Friday night and sometimes they didn't get back home until Monday morning, just in time to shower and to go off to work. Every now and then, the girls would get together and go to a club where they would meet other men. Somehow that was acceptable to them back in those days.

At one point, the federal government had a reduction-in-force, better known as a RIF, and my mother and most of her friends were laid off. She then got a job as a cocktail waitress at Highboys, where she met a woman named Arlene Cooper. They became very close friends quickly and enjoyed many years of friendship. Arlene became my brother's godmother. My mother was amused by Arlene because she never had any money to hand in at the end of the night. Arlene would get a $5.00 "bank" to make change every night at work but she ended up drinking with the men and spending the "bank" and all of her tips. My mother would cover for Arlene so she would not lose her job.

Our house was known as a party house. My parents would play those old 45 records with the holes in the middle. They played all kinds of music by different artists like Ray Charles, Johnny Ace, Dinah Washington, Lloyd Price, Brook Benton, Jackie Wilson, and Jerry Butler, just to name a few. Most of the songs had a fast beat and really helped to keep the party going.

Sometimes at these parties my parents would wake my brother and me so that we could show their friends our latest dance steps. We always complained about being awakened, but once we got on the dance floor we had a ball. Everyone thought it was so neat that my stepfather and I danced as if we had been dancing for years. We were like the black Fred Astaire and Ginger Rogers. Their friends actually applauded after we finished dancing.

My brother and I had to return to bed when the party albums started playing. The party albums were the 33's with dirty jokes on them. Our parents didn't want us to hear the albums, but they played them so loud we heard every word. During the week when they were at work, my brother and I would play the party records and take turns pretending to be Redd Foxx, Moms Mabley or Clay Tyson. We could tell some of the jokes better than the artists, but we didn't always know what they meant. A couple of times we play-acted a joke or two for our parents. They would laugh and ask us where we heard the joke. We would never say a word, but my stepfather would tell us he didn't want to find out we were playing those records.

Home Alone

There were times when we had to stay home alone while our parents went to someone else's house for a party. While they were gone, I was responsible for taking care of my brother. I remember being so scared I would hear every creak in the house. Sometimes my imagination would tell me that someone was trying to break in. My brother would stay up playing with his model cars, and he would fall asleep in his room with all the lights on. I would sit up waiting for my parents to come home wondering if they would come home happy or fighting.

When I was four or five years old, I began to wake up in the middle of the night seeing horrible dark colors spinning in the room. The colors were the same as a peacock's, but they were dark and ugly; not brilliant and beautiful at all. The more I saw the colors spin, the more I wanted to throw up. I began to realize I only saw these colors when my mother and my stepfather were fighting. These fights became more frequent and volatile as I got older. I learned very fast that the Lord could stop a fight in less than 10 minutes if I prayed hard enough.

The fights usually were the result of my stepfather's jealousy. He always suspected my mother of having affairs with other men, though he couldn't prove it. Truthfully, my mother was having affairs, but Matthew was not able to catch her. She was a firm believer that you never admit anything even if your husband put his hands on you right in the middle of an act. On the flip side of things, Matthew was also having affairs and had no problem admitting what he was doing.

Every Friday, we would eat out or go get some crabs, shrimp, or maybe something from the Hot Shoppe, a chain of restaurants that has long gone out of business. Liquor was always a must at every gathering. There were gallons of liquor in the house at all times. My parents always got drunk to the point that they would get sick the next morning, but they would start all over the next day. Often, their guests would have to sleep over if they drank too much, and they would be there when we woke up.

My brother's godmother Arlene would come and spend the weekend with us from time to time. At times, I believed her presence made Matthew be on his best behavior, although I remember him saying he thought Arlene was a "dike." My brother and I didn't care what she was; we just loved her and she was very good to us. One night she was visiting and had been drinking beer. She loved her beer. Of course, my stepfather drank hard liquor and after a few drinks, he decided to drive somewhere. He could never stay home. The man would always get behind the wheel of his car and go some place.

This particular night he and Arlene went out without my mother. While they were out riding around, I believe he made a pass at Arlene and she refused his advances. They got into a knock-down, drag-out fistfight in the middle of Georgia Avenue. I heard that Arlene was kicking his ass. After my stepfather realized his ass was being royally kicked, he jumped into his car and left Arlene standing in the middle of the street. She then called my mother to warn her because she knew what type of person he was. When he arrived home, he accused my mother of having an affair with Arlene and started beating her.

I ran next door to Mama M's, my after-school sitter, to call the police, and they came and arrested my stepfather. Of course, he had to go to jail and then to court. Funny enough, every time he had to go to court he would attend church the Sunday before his court date. At this particular hearing, he turned on the charm and put on a grand performance. When he finished, everyone believed his lies. Sometimes I had to shake my head in disbelief over how he could get away with his lying. Why couldn't people see through him? Unfortunately, my mother was too weak to speak up and tell the truth. On the rare occasion when she would speak up, no one believed her.

The Court Room Drama

Matthew told the judge that he thought Arlene was a "dike" and that he thought my mother was having an affair with her. The judge sided with him and told my mother to "keep her seahorses out of their house and things would be much better." I forgot what Arlene said and I can't remember what my mother said, either. I remember that I didn't really know what was going on during the court proceedings, but I know we didn't see Arlene again for a very long time.

In 1958, when I was eight years old, my mother became a part-time cab driver and continued driving cabs until her retirement in 1983. This job allowed her to visit friends or lovers whenever she wanted to and no one was the wiser. When Matthew thought she was seeing someone, he would demand to see her daily log of passengers and the amount of the fares that she collected. Mother never filled in the log correctly and that would only make him angrier. When he really got angry he would tell her to give him all the money she made that day. There was always chaos of some sort, and that was an example of how my mother and Matthew interacted on a regular basis. They were always lying and playing games with each other.

The way my mother and stepfather lived caused me to develop insecurities and a warped idea of what a relationship should be like. All the drinking and fighting took away my sense of stability and security, which every child should feel when growing up. I knew I could not rely on my parents, and I lived in fear that something bad was going to happen because they fought so much. Though I didn't know it at the time, I was experiencing emotional abuse and neglect.

The Beatings

The abuse was magnified at times when I did something my stepfather felt was wrong. If I did anything like write on the walls, or get a bad report card, I was told to go to the basement and remove all my clothes. Within five to seven minutes, which seemed like forever, my stepfather would appear and whip me with his belt. I always ended up urinating on myself, and that would make the beating worse. Once I tried to run away from him while he was beating me. He told me he would kill me if I ever tried to run again. I felt helpless after that and had to stand still and take my beatings as best I could.

Sometimes he would talk to me before starting to beat me. He would ask me over and over why I did whatever I did at that time. He would stare at my naked body too, and I would stand there feeling humiliated. I felt so bad. I wished he would hurry up and beat me and get it over with so I could go take a nice warm bath to soothe my pain. Every time I think of what happened, I still feel the shame of having to stand in front of him nude. Sometimes after my beatings he would tell me he was sorry. But yet he would continue to beat me the same way each time.

Soothing the Pain

I found out early in life that water was very soothing to me. Even now if I'm upset about something, I take a long hot bath and cry until I feel better. We all have to have a way to escape, and that has always been one of the healthier ways I cope with things. Bath time has always been a time when I could be alone to wash away the pain and heal myself. The baths soothed me both physically and emotionally.

CHAPTER 3
The Family Secret

When I was nine years old, I was on summer vacation at my maternal grandmother's house when my real father, and his second wife, Zelma, came to visit. Since I had never seen my father, I had no idea who he was. My grandmother had positioned me on the front porch and had given me a small chore to do to make sure my father could get a good look at me. The next morning, I asked my Aunt Joy who were the two people who came to visit the day before. She told me to ask my grandmother because she didn't want to be involved. So, I asked my grandmother, and she told me the truth. She told me that the man was my real father and she said that it was important that I promise that I never tell a living soul that I had seen him. That was when I discovered that Matthew Stevens, Sr. wasn't my real father. Although I had promised not to tell, I couldn't wait to get home to tell everybody the news.

One Saturday while my mother was at work, I told my stepfather that I had a secret that I couldn't tell him. He started to tickle me until I told him what I had known in my heart of hearts for years—that he was not my father. It was almost like I really wanted to hurt him for beating me and my mother. I knew that I could not have come from a man who was that crazy.

I will never forget that day, or the look on his face after I told him. He looked like he was angry and, at the same time, he looked a little sad. After that day, he never treated me the same. I remember him and my mother having a heated argument over my grandmother telling me the truth. He was angry with my grandmother, but he never told her that I revealed the secret. Later on, my mother told my grandmother that she did not appreciate her telling me about my real father.

The emotional confusion my mother created by not telling me about my real father was another form of abuse. I was forced to question my identity and why my real father didn't want to be with me. I was then rejected by my stepfather who was angry at being lied to and having to raise another man's child.

From that point on, things changed. My stepfather stopped buying nice clothes for me. I received only one gift from him at Christmas. The last thing I got from him was a heart-shaped pendant with a little diamond chip in the middle that he gave me in 1961. Then the beatings got longer and much harder. To make matters worse, the children at school began to tease me about the welts on my legs.

Rejection

As a result of my stepfather's rejection, I became more vocal. I would speak up whenever there was a fight or whenever he did something I didn't like. In my mind, the war was on and I no longer cared what came out of my mouth. I found courage to speak up for my mother and myself. When her beatings were really bad, she would have to go to the hospital, and I would go with her. We endured the same old cycle of a fight, an arrest by the police, a court date and a court appearance. Each time my stepfather would lie like he believed God was on his side. Each time he would return home without punishment. In the end, we became more afraid of him and what he would do because we knew he could get away with it.

At one point, I was so angry at him that I tried to poison him by putting bug spray in his water glass. He'd asked me to get a glass of cold water for him because he was dehydrated from a weekend drunk. I sprayed the bug spray in the glass, but my mother saw me and took the glass away from me. She told me that I would go to hell for trying to poison him. My mother always said God would take care of him, but I wondered when that would happen. I felt God needed some help.

I have always felt a sense of freedom from being able to read. I used to go through my mother's important papers in the bottom of her dresser drawer and read them. One day I found some legal papers pertaining to my mother's divorce from my biological father and my stepfather's divorce from his previous wife. Among those papers, I found my birth certificate which clearly stated who my birth father was. It was the proof I needed that what my grandmother said was true.

CHAPTER 4
The Start of Sexual Abuse

I've been told by three mediums that I was sexually assaulted at a very early age. I didn't remember being abused, nor did I want to remember. In the back of my mind, I always knew it was so, but I was too ashamed to admit it to anyone, even my psychiatrist, and I trusted her. But on the other hand, I thought sexual abuse meant someone had intercourse with you. I now know that sexual abuse is not always as overt as that. Childhood sexual abuse encompasses many acts performed by an adult onto a child. I developed at a very early age, and I have clear memory of my stepfather fondling my breasts when I was around the age of eight or nine. The fondling was very uncomfortable, and I wanted it to stop. After six months or so, I decided that the next time he touched me, I would take whatever I could get my hands on and beat him with it.

About two weeks after making that promise to God and myself, he fondled my breasts again. I quickly reacted by picking up a Teflon skillet and hitting him with all the strength I had in me. I had never felt such rage and such hatred. If I could have killed him, I would have, and I'm sure I would not have felt any remorse. Later that day, I heard him tell my mother, "That girl really hurt my shoulder." My mother replied that it was time for him to stop. At that time, my body was maturing into young adulthood and very soon after that I started my period. It was March 10, 1960. I was nine years old.

My parents continued to fight over the same old shit. I lived in constant fear that my stepfather would kill my mother or that he would lose it with me. I became increasingly stressed by my home environment, and consequently, my grades started becoming U's instead of D's and C's. The situation at home was really interfering with my ability to learn. Of course, I got a beating for not bringing home a good report card.

No one understood the reasons behind the bad grades or my frequent outbursts of crying. I remember trying to talk to one of my elementary school counselors and friends about what was going on, but I'm not sure they understood me. No one intervened on my behalf, though I'm sure they could see the signs of abuse. There I was, an innocent child of God, with no one there to protect me from the sickness in my family.

CHAPTER 5
Family Dysfunction

My stepfather came home one night while my mother was out with a friend of the family. He asked where she was, and I told him she was with Jasper Clemons. He then called Jasper's house, but no one answered the phone. He took a drink and went to find my mother. When they got back, all I could hear was, "Baby don't hit me." He was accusing her of having an affair with Jasper. My mother tried to tell him he was crazy, but that only made him angrier. He suddenly took a carving knife out of the kitchen drawer and started beating her with it. It was the worse beating I had ever seen my mother get.

Matthew then dialed Jasper's telephone number, asked for him by name, and gave the phone to my mother. He tried to catch her in a lie by listening in on the conversation. While she was talking, he suddenly snatched the receiver from her hand and hit her in her face with it. She screamed so loudly I thought he was killing her. When he finished, she had a black eye from where he hit her with the telephone receiver, and he had also bitten a piece of the flesh from her back. The fight seemed to go on forever. I kept thinking he was going to kill her for sure, and it would be my fault. After the fight was over, my mother had to go to the hospital for stitches and a tetanus shot. The next day, I heard him threaten to beat her again if she didn't admit she had been with Jasper. I always felt guilty for that particular beating. I felt responsible because I told on her. It bothers me to think about it even today.

A few days later, my mother took me to the bank with her to make a deposit. I remember that she was still stiff and sore with a lot of visible bruises. She questioned me out loud in front of everyone at the bank about telling Matthew where she was. She expected me to cover for her in the future.

A month later, my mother and Matthew were acting like nothing had ever happened. I, however, blamed myself for years and never seemed to get over it. I had been mentally programmed to believe I was responsible.

Part of the anger I felt as a child was over being used as a scapegoat and being put in the middle of my parents' issues. I was expected to lie, be peacemaker and to be a part-time parent for my brother, thanks to my parents' crazy lifestyle. I was also angry at my mother for not being the wife and mother I thought she should be. My mother had been leaving me to take care of my brother since I was seven or eight years old. No child should have to play that role at such a young age. My thinking became more and more distorted by their behavior because I was taught how to play games with people emotionally. Children should be protected from dysfunction, but I was used by both my parents as a pawn in the games they played with each other.

The Questioning

It was nothing for Matthew to turn on the lights in my room when I was fast asleep, wake me and question me about what my mother was doing. He rarely questioned my brother about her. I had to learn how to lie to protect my mother and myself or there would be consequences. In fact, I got so good at lying to cover up things that it became automatic. I remember him asking me where my mother was one night while I was trying to sleep, and I told him she was at a PTA meeting at my school. Later that night, he woke me a second time and asked the same question, and I looked him straight in the eyes and said, "She's at my school attending a PTA meeting."

CHAPTER 6
It Is Never the Child's Fault

After years of working with my psychiatrist, I know without a doubt that none of the things that happened to me was my fault. Dr. Welsing told me that I lived in a war zone and that I needed to recognize that I was not the adult in control. I was only a child. I now understand that most of my childhood was taken away from me. For a long time, there was a part of me that felt responsible for my family's unhappiness. My parents had me convinced that I was the cause of the problems in the family, and I felt that if I had not been born, my parents would have been happier. Every beating I suffered reinforced my belief that I was bad and unlovable.

The Victim Role

There are so many things that happened to me when I played that victim role. I believe that when you have been abused, other abusers sense it and pick up right where the last abuser left off. In other words, the abused person starts to attract other abusers. My boundaries had been violated, and my understanding of what love was had been distorted. I wanted someone to love me, so I tried to find love from anyone I thought would give me the attention I so desperately needed. I now have tools to recognize abusers, and now I get away from them. I feel I am spiritually protected from unhealthy men because I have invited God into my life and my heart. I know what love really is, and I no longer allow abusers to take advantage of me.

Looking for Love in all the Wrong Places

People used to tell me I was well beyond my age mentally and physically. For that reason I think it was easy for older people to forget that I was still a child. By the time I was 12 years old, I was having sexual intercourse with a 36-year old married man named Harold who worked at the post office not far from where I lived. He was what they call a pedophile today.

I would go to the post office for Mama M to purchase stamps and mail packages. Because I went there regularly, this man started developing a friendship with me. I remember telling him about my home life because I trusted him. He pretended to be a father figure to me in the beginning, and I felt safe with him and felt that he would never hurt me. He earned my trust by being attentive to me and what I had to say. He even taught me how to roller skate.

One day he told me he was being transferred to another post office. I cried and told him that I loved him and didn't want to see him go. That's when the little wrestling matches started. Before long, he was tugging at my clothes as I fought to keep them on. Eventually he raped me in his car. I remember how painful it was that first time, but in spite of the pain, I felt I was doing something that was normal because grownups did it. I remember always wanting to be an adult, but I didn't realize at that time that I just wasn't ready for sexual intercourse.

Harold always used a condom. He said he was protecting me, but in reality, he was protecting himself. There was no enjoyment in having sex at that time in my life. I didn't know what the hell I was doing. At the same time, I was afraid of losing the affection that Harold gave me. He called me his "choc cherry," which was short for chocolate cherry. That was his way of saying he had taken my virginity. He liked to remind me of that every chance he could.

They say you always love the first person you have sex with, and I thought I loved Harold. He had done what all pedophiles do by playing on my vulnerability and need to feel loved. Instead of being a protector and friend like I needed, he crossed boundaries by taking the relationship to a physical level. I did not understand the effect that would have on my life. It set a pattern for allowing other men to cross my boundaries, which continued for many years.

My aunt Claire knew that I was having sexual intercourse with Harold, and she also crossed boundaries. She used that information to her advantage later on when I really needed her help.

In November 1962, at the age of 12, my stepfather's mother died in a car accident. Of course, we went to New Jersey as a family to plan her funeral. Aunt Claire brought a woman with her to help with the driving. en it was time for bed, I was told to sleep in the living room with woman. My aunt slept in one room, and my parents and my brother slept in another room. Sometime in the middle of the night, this woman started fondling my breasts and kissing me all over my body. Yes, my body responded to the pleasure, but my mind said it was wrong. This was very frightening to me. I never told anyone about this incident. It took me years to come to the realization that this woman did the same thing the men in my life had done. This still bothers me more than anything else that has happened to me. Why, because in my mind, I probably haven't fully come to terms with it.

CHAPTER 7
Reacting to the Abuse

As time passed, I was very unhappy at home and started to become rebellious. My grades were not good, and I became angrier and angrier. I started trying to get back at my stepfather by leaving notes around that said, "My name is Hilda Thomasine Wren." That was my way of pushing his buttons emotionally. The notes always pissed him off, which is exactly the reaction I was looking for.

I began spending more time in the school counselor's office trying to get support, but I always had a hard time explaining my feelings. I never knew what to expect when I got home or what kind of mood Matthew would be in when he got there. I was in constant emotional turmoil. At that time, I did not realize that Harold had added to the turmoil by taking advantage of me. I was completely ignorant of the fact that I had been taken advantage of and I was completely confused by the relationship. I did not know what a sexually healthy relationship was all about and began to confuse sex with love. I thought my family life was the cause of all my misery when it really was a combination of my home life and my relationship with Harold.

My parents expected me to make my bed and theirs every day before going to school as part of my chores. I also had to mop the kitchen, dust the furniture in their bedroom, put the dishes in the dishwasher, cut the grass, and clean and wax the hardwood floors in the living room and dining room. Cleaning the hardwood floors was only done twice a year, but it was still hard work. I was also told to come home by 3:30 p.m., and I received a daily phone call from my stepfather to make sure I was there and doing my chores.

Though I didn't like having chores, I knew that it was a good thing to be given responsibilities at home. The part that was upsetting for me was that my stepfather would get angry at me if he didn't feel I had done a good job. He always seemed to get mad at me for not dusting his room well enough. In his words, "If you dusted why is the furni still dusty?" Then he would wipe his hand over one of the end tables to show me what he was talking about. Years later, I understood I couldn't keep the furniture dust free because my parents' windows were always open, especially during the spring and early summer. Since the windows were always open, the pollen would continually blow in and cover the furniture.

CHAPTER 8
Being Abandoned by My Father

My eighth grade Personal Family Living teacher (PFL) at McFarland Jr. High School was Mrs. Evelyn Jones. She called me aside one day and asked me if I knew Lawrence Wren. I told her I had only seen him once, but knew who he was. She told me that as long as I lived he would live. Of course, I asked her what that meant and she said, "Child, you look just like him."

A Plea for Help

Out of desperation to get away from my situation at home, I tried to contact my real father. His phone number was listed in the phone book, so I called and asked to speak to him. His wife Zelma always told me he was busy or was at work. When she questioned why I was calling, I always told her that I just needed to speak with him. She never let me talk to him. At some point, I did tell Zelma why I was calling. I told her about my life at home and that I wanted my father's help. I'm not sure if she ever told him that I called because he never responded to the calls and made no effort to help me.

CHAPTER 9
Scared Stiff

One day I was feeling anxious and worried about everything, yet I wasn't able to explain what was going on in my mind or body. I sensed that there was about to be another big fight or argument. I was always waiting for the next shoe to drop, especially if it was close to my birthday, Thanksgiving, or Christmas. At those times my stepfather really got drunk and showed his ass. I was so worried, that I couldn't think about anything but leaving school. I called Aunt Claire on my lunch break and asked if I could come to her house. She always had a way of making you think things were better than they really were. She would have music playing, and I would be able to forget about my problems while I was at her house. I took a cab to her house, and she paid the fare for me.

My aunt ran a house of prostitution in those days. There was always plenty of food, liquor, women, music and johns who were willing to spend their hard-earned money on a nice tender woman. A man could not sit in her house without spending some money.

When I arrived, Aunt Claire greeted me at the door and asked, "Why do you look so down?" I told her I had no idea, but that I wanted to run away because I was tired of all of the craziness at home. We talked until it was past the time for me to be home. The more time went on, the more scared and nervous I became because I knew my stepfather would be calling to check on me. At that point, I knew it wouldn't be safe for me to go home. I would get a beating if I did.

A Runaway Teenager

After Aunt Claire found out that I was serious about running away, she called Harold at the post office to see if he could talk some sense into me. Six o'clock came, and I made up my mind I would stay at her house that night. When my mother called to see if I was there, my aunt lied and said she had not seen me. The next day Aunt Claire told me I had to go.

By that time the police had been called. An announcement had been made on a local radio station, asking people to call in if they had seen me. Harold called Aunt Claire that morning and said he had heard the announcement on the radio. He wanted me to go home, but I was too scared to go and decided to visit Matthew and Claire's stepfather/uncle in New Jersey, instead.

I always thought this man was my grandfather and no one ever explained who he really was. Granddaddy McFadden, as we called him, had just accidentally driven his car into a tree. He had been drinking and driving, and his wife Phyllis died in the crash. He had just come home from the hospital, recovering from multiple injuries not long before I called and asked if I could visit him.

I got money from Aunt Claire and decided to take a Trailways bus to Camden, New Jersey where my grandfather lived. Little did I know that the bus didn't go directly to Camden. It went to Newark, and I had to take a commuter bus back to Camden. I was so scared. I arrived in the middle of rush hour traffic, and it was so dark and cold. There I was standing in my high heels, looking lost and afraid. I didn't know anyone in Newark, but the bus driver was nice enough to drop me off where I could catch a cab to my grandfather's house.

When I arrived, my grandfather greeted me with open arms. Deep down, he suspected that there were problems in each of his children's homes. Apparently my aunt had called to warn him that I was on my way because he had called my parents before I arrived. When I got there, I was very tired and hungry, but I was only able to eat a little because my stomach was all tied in knots. Everything I tried to eat felt as if it was going to come back up. I fell asleep as soon as my head hit the pillow that night.

The next day my parents arrived very upset, but glad to see that I was okay. My stepfather didn't say very much until we were in the car and on our way home. Then he told me that the next time I ran away, I'd better keep running. He said he was never coming after me again.

My mother explained to me why they came to get me instead of the police. Since I had left the Washington, D.C. area, I was considered a runaway, and if the police had transported me back home from New Jersey, I would have had a record and would have to go to court. Unconsciously, I think I was trying to get into trouble as a way to reach out for help. Going to court might have gotten me the help I needed.

When we got into D.C., my parents stopped at the Hot Shoppes to get my favorite meal—a teenwist, fries and an orange freeze. I enjoyed every bite, but it came back up as soon as I got home. I got on the scale and saw that I had lost six pounds in less than three days. My mother said my coloring was not good at all and I had shadows under my eyes.

The Return Home

The next day, I went next door to Mama M's to see my best friend Zepora. Mama M and Zepora were Seventh Day Adventists and were very caring and loving towards me. Zepora was six years older than I, and she and Mama M understood what I was going through at home. They could hear all the turmoil in our house when my parents were fighting.

Zepora was excited to see me and rushed me up to her room to ask me the details of my runaway experience. She also gave me some bad news. My mother had been very upset and was crying because she could not find me. She asked Zepora if she knew where I was, and Zepora told her about Harold. They called information, got his address, and went over to his house. My mother told his wife that I had mentioned to her that they, as a couple, had taken an interest in me and she just wanted to know if she had any idea where I was. The lady had no idea what my mother was talking about.

While Zepora and my mother were there, Harold called home from work to see if his wife needed anything from the store. She told him "no" but to hurry home because she had a surprise waiting for him. A year later, Harold told me he almost passed out when he opened the door and spotted my mother and Zepora sitting in his living room talking to his wife. At that point, our sexual relationship was officially over.

Harold and I didn't see each other again for years, but we did talk from time to time over the phone. About five or six years later, I went to see him at the Columbia Heights post office and we sat and talked. Someone in my family had died, and I went to see him because I was sad and thought talking to him would help. He told me that his brother was serving time for rape and carnal knowledge that took place during the same time Harold was raping me. Of course, Harold didn't use the word rape, but I'm using that term now because I now know that is what he was doing to me. He raped me every chance he could get. He also told me his wife called all of their relatives and told them about what happened between us.

The legal term for what Harold did to me as a minor is *statutory rape.* I can now call it what it was. Harold used my vulnerability against me. He knew I had a difficult home life, and he made me feel like he cared about me so he could take advantage of me. He raped me from 1963 to

1965. I was 12 years old when it all began. He has never apologized or taken responsibility for his actions towards me.

After I returned home, things were almost normal. I don't know whose idea it was for me to see a psychiatrist, but I started seeing one at Georgetown University Hospital's Clinic. After several appointments with the doctors, my mother was told to bring her husband into the office. They realized he was the root of the problem, not me. Matthew refused to go to any of the appointments until years later.

The Baby Sitting Job

When I was approximately 13-years old, I was told to baby-sit the children of one of my parents' friends. They all went out to a party together. It was very late that night when the children's father returned home alone. I thought he came back to check on the children who were asleep. Instead, he started kissing on me. I remember the awful smell of alcohol on his breath. He removed me from his sofa and placed me on the floor where he started fondling me. Then he tried to have intercourse with me without removing my underwear, which caused my body to react to the stimuli with pleasure, but my mind was saying "no." There were no words spoken between us at all. I was so glad when one of his children woke up and started crying and he left in a hurry. I was so nervous I couldn't sleep for weeks as my mind kept replaying the events of that night.

I often wondered if my stepfather had told his friend that I was not his child. What other reason would a man, supposedly a family friend, take advantage of me in that way. I refuse to believe he did all that just because he was under the influence of alcohol.

To this day, that man continues to harass me. I have had to threaten to tell his children about his behavior to get him to leave me alone. The person I am today cannot let him get away with continuing to try to victimize me.

The Restaurant

When I was 15 or 16, a classy new seafood restaurant, Road House Inn, opened up in D.C. My parents and I went the first Friday it opened. I was dressed in a very nice navy blue dress with navy blue leather heels. My parents had been drinking and because the glass doors were clean and clear, my mother walked right into them. The restaurant was so new they had not put the monograms on the glass doors. I remember the glass sounding like a bell as it shook from the impact. My mother wasn't hurt, but it was very embarrassing.

We were seated and our waiter brought water and a basket of rolls with butter. I guess my stepfather was very hungry because he started right in with the rolls. My mother and I were talking about how beautiful the place was when I noticed that my stepfather was buttering the small lamp on the table. We laughed ourselves silly. Then my stepfather wanted to use the men's room. He yelled out to the waiter, who was way across the room, "Come here!" I quietly said to my stepfather, "You shouldn't yell." The waiter came, and we thought he escorted my stepfather to the men's room. When my stepfather returned, he told us in the loudest voice he could that the men's room had not been completed and he had to go across the street to urinate in a parking lot. All those nicely dressed white folks were looking at us. I guess they were wondering, "Where in the hell did these people come from?"

CHAPTER 10
My Life as a Prostitute

Even though I was told not to visit Aunt Claire, I went anyway. I would go over to her house just to get away from the craziness at my house. I needed a place to relax, and I had nowhere else to go. On Saturdays, I would lie and say that I was going shopping downtown. One day while I was at my aunt's house, she asked a guy if he wanted to see something real pretty. She told him it would cost him $10.00. Little did I know that she was talking about my breasts. I remember that she was standing behind me while she was talking to this man. All of a sudden she pulled my sweater up around my head, and my entire chest was exposed. The man jumped up, threw a twenty-dollar bill on the table and stated he had not seen anything that pretty and tender in a long while. Aunt Claire laughed at me for being so embarrassed and gave me $5.00. From that day on, if I asked her for any money, she would tell me that I was sitting on money. The money was between my legs, and all I had to do was get off it and not be so lazy. She also told me I had been giving it away, so I might as well make some money with it. After asking her for money several times and being refused, I started selling my body. By that time, I learned that opening my legs got me money and attention and my boundaries were almost non-existent. I found myself doing things without caring about how it was affecting me.

My first john was a congressman, and I was 13-years old. Johns are customers. I didn't know at the time he was a congressman. He had an apartment in the Washington suburbs.

I got out of school a half day and went to Aunt Claire's house to take a quick bath, put on perfume, and primp. I took a cab to the apartment and was greeted at the door by the doorman. When I arrived at the congressman's apartment, this very handsome man opened the door and asked me to be seated. He offered me a drink and a cigarette and I refused. He talked about everything under the sun. I had always been able to make people think I understood everything they were saying, but

I usually didn't understand jack shit. I didn't have to say a thing, so I just nodded my head in the affirmative from time to time. He showed me his bedroom, and I undressed and got into his bed. He took full control of the situation from then on. When it was all over he paid me $150.00, plus cab fare. I got to keep $75.00, and my aunt got the other half. I never saw him again. Later on Aunt Claire told me that he was one of her regulars, and I was sent as a little treat for him.

The next john was a white guy who was real skinny. He smelled just like a wet dog. He had a very short and skinny penis and fucked real fast like a rabbit. He was the first person who made me reach a climax. I always wondered how the hell he was able to do that. I especially didn't understand it because I didn't like him. I thought you had to be in love with a person before they could make you get off. Every time this man came to Aunt Claire's house, he expected to see me. After seeing him a half dozen times and others in between him, I thought I knew something about sex. By that time, I felt I knew how to at least satisfy a man. "Oh, how dumb could I be?" Little did I know there was more to just fucking in the missionary position.

A month later Aunt Claire set me up with another white guy. He was a salesman of some sort. He probably sold insurance. Back then the insurance man came to your house to pick up your monthly payment. I met this guy at her house just as I met all of the other johns. His name was Sid, and she told us to use her middle bedroom since her six kids were in school. That's where I should have been.

Sid got undressed before me and jumped right into the bed. I thought it was so funny he never took off his socks. I took my clothes off but had a feeling something wasn't right. I ignored the feeling. Before I knew it, Sid had his penis in my vagina fucking me. The next minute his penis was in my mouth. I had tasted my own juices. I thought to myself, "Oh God I'm going to be sick." I wanted to stop. Sweat was coming out of every pore in my body. Then I became dizzy and I gagged. He was holding my head down and forcing his penis in and out of my mouth. Then, as he came in my mouth, he said to me, "You are a good bitch," and he let my head go. I ran to the bathroom and threw up. I tasted the nasty, salty taste of his semen, and I thought I would die. By the time I stopped throwing up and got myself cleaned up, I heard Sid and Aunt Claire laughing in her dining room. I wondered if they were laughing at me. I thought, "What was so damn funny?" The experience was so horrible that I was shaking, and I didn't see anything to laugh about.

I stayed upstairs until Aunt Claire said that Sid was gone. After that incident, I didn't go over to her house for a month or two. I couldn't believe what had happened to me. Even today, the whole incident is still very fresh in my mind. The memory still makes me want to vomit. I just thank God AIDS was not out then.

Disassociation

The next time I turned a trick, I closed my mind, shut my eyes, and became numb. My doctors told me that I disassociated from my body. The next few johns did not require me to "French" them, or—in today's terms—give a man a blowjob. Harold tried to guide my head in that direction on several occasions, but I put up such a good fight that he never forced the issue. Sid had really caught me off guard.

My Aunt's Boyfriend

Aunt Claire told me her new boyfriend Warren was excellent in bed and she wanted me to share that experience with him. I don't remember if I openly agreed, but I remember thinking, "Why would she do that if he is her boyfriend?"

I had just bathed and was in Aunt Claire's room getting dressed when Warren walked in. He was tall, dark, and handsome with a nice-sized penis. He gently placed me on the bed and started kissing me from head to toe. He even kissed and lingered around the clitoris area. I thought that I was in heaven and I reached a full-blown climax by the time he finished kissing me. Never mind the fucking, the oral sex was more than enough. Then, he starting fucking me and boy was it good. Before I knew what had happened, I had reached another climax. I have not found anyone to satisfy me like that since. I've found a few men who have come close, but no one like Warren.

CHAPTER 11
Continuing Chaos

As usual, the fights were still going on at our house. I became more distant with my immediate family and my surroundings. Remembering that fights were worse just before my birthday and during the Thanksgiving and Christmas holidays, I understand why I still get sad just before my birthday and continue to stay sad until after the New Year.

My stepfather always accused me of the same things he accused my mother of doing. Once my mother was late getting home, and he was walking around the outside of the house looking for her with a pistol in his hand. He asked me if she had called during the day, and then he pointed the gun at me and told me he was going to kill me after he killed her. He said I was no good just like her. He didn't kill my mother, but she got an ass beating that night for getting home late. My stepfather expected her to be home every night by 6:00 p.m.

Skipping School

Months passed and I continued to prostitute myself to the same old men whenever I could skip school. I played hooky nine times in one semester. One day, the assistant principal called me into her office and asked me why I was missing school so much. She wanted to know if there was a problem. I told her no and she said she would be calling my mother that day during my lunch period. I ran home for lunch and waited for the phone to ring. When it did, I answered it and the assistant principal asked for Mrs. Stevens. I replied, "This is Mrs. Stevens." She explained that I had missed nine days and wanted an explanation. I told her that I was shocked and would take care of the situation immediately. I assured her that Hilda would not be able to sit down after I got finished with her. I told no one what I did, not even my best girlfriend.

How I Spent the Money

At any given time, I had anywhere between a hundred and a hundred and fifty dollars from prostituting. I was so afraid that my stepfather would find the money, because he was forever looking in my dresser drawers to see if I had hidden anything, and he read my mail and my diary.

I gave some of my money to Aunt Claire to purchase clothes for me from time to time. She would always pretend that she was downtown and saw this or that that she knew I'd love. Then, she would drop by our house with the "gifts." Now that I think back on it, I wonder why no one became suspicious. After all, she had six children of her own. The question that should have been asked is, "Why was she always buying clothes for someone else's child?"

I spent some of the money giving parties at my house for my cousins and their friends. I remember giving a Christmas party the year James Brown released "Lets Make This Christmas Mean Something This Year." Another time, I decided to host a picnic in Rock Creek Park. I bought the food, cooked, and invited everyone to come and enjoy themselves. The next summer, I gave a picnic on a Sunday afternoon and asked Aunt Claire to come. She said that she had to stay home to make some money, but she asked her next door neighbors, Mr. and Mrs. Cook, if they would take us and be the adult chaperones for us teens. We were all enjoying the food, dancing, and telling dirty jokes. Around 7:00 p.m., I asked Mr. Cook if he could take me home before dark, and come back later on to pick up the others. You see, the rule in my household was that my brother and I had to be home before the street lights came on. Since my cousins were older, my aunt didn't care what time they came home.

Mr. Cook agreed to take me home, and I went over to my cousin Ray to say goodbye. Approximately five or 10 minutes later, I heard Mrs. Cook saying, "Ain't no coming back. Ain't no coming back." I heard her speaking, but had no idea what was going on. Ray was seated where he could see everything, and all of a sudden, he picked me up and rushed me to the other side of the park. Once we had some distance between Mrs. Cook and us, we started us, I turned around and saw that Mr. Cook was trying to take a straight razor from his wife. He fought her for several minutes, and he took the razor from her and immediately took her home.

Ray explained to me that Mrs. Cook was mentally ill, and she thought I was after her man. If Mr. Cook had not stopped her, I would not be here today. As a good friend told me, "Your angels were working triple time to keep you alive."

As I think back on that incident, I remember that Mrs. Cook was a homemaker whenever she was not in the hospital for her illness. I am sure she saw me going into Aunt Claire's house when I should have been in school. Everyone in my aunt's neighborhood knew what she did for a living, therefore, Mrs. Cook probably assumed I was trying to get a date with her husband.

CHAPTER 12
My First Job

During the summer of 1965, at age 14, I got my first summer job working for a dance studio as a telephone solicitor. I enjoyed calling people and asking them if they wanted to learn how to dance. For a while, I did the job well until one day I got bored and started calling people and playing practical jokes on them. For example, I would call a liquor store and ask if they had Prince Albert in the can. And, when they said yes, I would say, "Damn man, it's hot in there. Let him out." Then I'd hang up the phone real fast. Or, I would call people at home and ask if their refrigerator was running and when they said "yes," I would say, "You better go catch it." I had all the women in my little section doing it. It was fun and it made the day go by faster. What I did not know was that the supervisor, Gina, monitored our conversations from time to time. I was caught, and Gina pulled me into her office. When she tried to call me on the carpet for it, I told her I could get them in trouble because I was under age. She sent me out that day and had me get a student work permit. I stayed with Arthur Murray's until the last week of August.

I met a guy who was in the Navy during the same time I was working for the dance studio. The guy's name was Charles. He had just turned 19 and I was 14. I met him at my aunt's house. He was a friend of her oldest son, Ray. We went out on several dates to the movies and to house parties. Every time we would go out, he insisted on having sex. He would use a new condom every time we had intercourse. If we had sex two times that night, he used two condoms. Charles was accustomed to someone giving him a blowjob before fucking. I went along with what he wanted because he was insistent, and I wanted to please him. I became an expert cocksucker under his directions. I never really enjoyed it, but it pleased him. I thought that was what I was there for, to please a man. No one ever taught me to put myself first and do what was right for me.

Charles thought he was in love, so I decided to be honest with him about my life at Aunt Claire's house. He made me feel real ashamed of myself, but a few days later he proposed marriage with the ring in his hand. Now that I think about it, he may have been trying to save me from my aunt, or maybe from myself.

I met his parents and I believed they liked me. Charles' father was a security guard in one of the government buildings in downtown D.C. His mother was a housewife. They took my brother and me on a trip to Luray Caverns in Virginia while Charles was stationed in Michigan. We had a lovely time. A few days later, I called Charles' house to thank them again for taking us, but when Charles' father answered the phone he asked me to call back. He said that his wife was busy, and she could not talk to me at that time. Later on, one of Charles' brothers called me and said his mother had died. Their father had found her on the floor in a diabetic coma.

Charles came home and I went to the wake and funeral with him. They were Catholic. I had never been to a Catholic funeral before. All I remember was kneeling for prayer and saying a bunch of "Hail Mary's." While Charles was home on leave, we went out to the movies and visited some of his old friends from school. And, of course, we had sex. He asked me if I had been over to my aunt's house selling pussy. I told him "no." I felt it was no one's business what I was doing.

Then one day, one of Charles' old girlfriends called him and told him she had something important to tell him. When he went to see what she wanted, she told him she was pregnant with his child. Charles came straight to me to ask what I thought he should do. He told me that they had been with each other before he met me, and he had broken off the relationship right around that same time. He broke down and cried, and he said he wished his mother were there so she could tell him what to do. I put my arms around him and whispered in his ear, "Charles, marry her. It is the only thing left to do." He laid his head in my arms on my front porch and cried like a baby.

After he got himself together he asked me for the ring so he would not have to purchase another one. I gave it to him and wished him well. I knew then that I didn't love him. The marriage between the two of us would not have lasted because Charles drank like a fish and would get a little rough with me every now and then. Also, I knew he would never trust me because of my aunt. Believe me when I tell you, God takes care of babies and fools.

Right after I broke up with Charles, I made up my mind that I would never tell another living soul about my secret life. No one ever needed to know my business, especially anyone who meant anything to me. I started working again at Aunt Claire's house approximately two weeks later and ended up seeing the same old regulars while I was there.

Working for Mr. Austin

In the summer of 1966, when I was 15, Aunt Claire told me that a friend of hers needed a secretary to work in his office for the summer. She introduced me to him at her house. He was Mr. Clifton Austin of Austin and Austin Construction Co. He told me he needed a secretary who could type a little, answer the phones, take messages and make out the payroll checks. He took one look at me and I had the job. Mr. Austin was a chain smoking, stinky old man. I worked for him the full summer and made pretty good money.

Aunt Claire told Mr. Austin that I was good in bed, and soon I was seeing him at her place. I had to give that man a bath before I could bring myself to fuck him and he still smelled bad. All the soap, cologne or powder in the world wouldn't make him smell any better. My aunt used to beg me to see him. I told her he had to pay me $100.00 each and every time I had sex with him. Even after I started charging $100.00, he continued to ask for me instead of the white chicks who worked the place.

Racial Tension and the Seventies

In the fall of 1966, at the age of 15, I obtained a job with the D.C. school system working with Project Head Start under the direction of my good pastor Rev. Dr. E. Singleton. I worked with some very nice and caring people whose influence kept me away from my aunt's house for a while. Dr. Singleton was running for D.C. committeeman and I helped campaign for him. On the day of the election, I held a sign with "Vote for Dr. E. Singleton" written on it in front of the Scottish Rites Mason's building. That was where I met Jeffrey Conner. Jeffrey's full time job was with Local Union #1. He talked all day about what he would do if he won a seat on the board. He had high hopes for the school system.

At the end of the day, my pastor had won a second term as a D.C. committeeman. Jeffrey and I exchanged telephone numbers and vowed to keep in touch, but we never talked after that day.

During those years, we had men like Jeffrey Conner, Julius Hobson, Rev. Doug Moore, Rev. Jesse Jackson, and other strong black men to look up to. I will never forget when my stepfather took me to the March on Washington on August 28, 1963 where Doctor Martin Luther King spoke. My mother dressed me in a bright red and white dress so that I would not get lost in the enormous crowd. Many of the celebrities from around the world were there to show their support. We all gathered around to listen to Dr. King's speech, and even though I didn't understand exactly what he was saying, I remember the awesome feeling of togetherness moving through the crowds. Of course, the march ended with that famous song "We Shall Overcome."

CHAPTER 13
Meeting Simon

In the summer of 1967, at age 16, I met Simon Benton. Simon and his brothers lived in South Carolina with his grandparents while his mother worked for the federal government. He and his brothers would come here for the summers to visit their mother. His mother's name was Bertha Benton, better known as Birdie. One day Birdie called and asked my mother if one of my girlfriends and I could take Simon and his friend Joseph out to do some sightseeing. My girlfriend Rosa was interested and we double dated all summer with those two very nice guys. I had my eyes on Joseph and hoped Rosa had her eyes on Simon, but it did not work out like I wanted it to. I got stuck with Simon who was very "green," which was the slang for a naïve person.

At the end of the summer, Joseph went back to South Carolina and Simon stayed here to find a job. He started working for George Washington Hospital as an orderly. We continued to date and had a lot of fun. We often visited each other's churches for Sunday service and had dinner at his mother's house or my mother's house afterwards. They were Baptist while we were Methodist.

Simon's birthday was August 19th, and I surprised him with a picnic lunch at a park. I also seduced him there, and he fell head over heels in love with me. We were together for more than two years. During that time, I was still going to my aunt's house to make money.

One night Simon's sister-in-law, Janice, was here visiting from South Carolina while waiting to join her husband in Germany. We invited her to the movies with us. While the movie played, Simon and I left and went to a tourist home around the corner from the theater. We made love there and by that time he was getting pretty good at it. Something happened when he reached his climax, which happened quickly for him. He mumbled, "Please, God don't let her get pregnant." At the time, I didn't think anything of what he said.

CHAPTER 14
My Grandmother's Passing

My grandmother became seriously ill in 1965. My stepfather didn't raise as much hell during the time my grandmother was ill, but he still drank like a fish. My mother was spending most of her time at my grandmother's house taking care of her while my stepfather was supposed to be taking care of my brother and me. He would get drunk, but there was not as much arguing going on since my mother was away from home so much. I stayed in my room and my brother stayed outside until the street lights came on.

Approximately one month before my grandmother died, my stepfather bought a brand new 1967 Buick Rivera. It was bronze and black with power windows and cruise control. The week he brought the car home, he slapped me in my face for something I did or said. I don't remember why he hit me, but I remember the next thing out of my mouth was, "You will wreck that car before the week ends." Saturday came and he decided to go see my mother, since she could not come home. He took off with the usual cooler of beer and a half gallon of gin, and he ended up at my grandmother's house a little high. Aunt Joy and her husband Andrew and my mother's brother Aaron were there.

My stepfather wanted to show off his new car, so he and my two uncles went for a ride. From what I have been told, he wanted to demonstrate how the cruise control worked. He set it on a short stretch of road, and when he tried to stop the car before the road ended, he pressed the accelerator instead of the brakes. Needless to say, they crashed into an embankment and the car turned over and landed on its roof. It was totaled.

Uncle Aaron was in the back seat. He saw the accident coming so he tried to get on his knees on the floor of the car. He wasn't fast enough, and he said a spring from the seat hit him in his ass. Uncle Andrew was up front with Matthew. He ended up with a terrible gash on the front of his leg and received over 27 stitches to close it. My stepfather hit his head on the windshield swelling it even bigger than it already was. The hospital wanted to keep him overnight for observation, but he refused stating that he was a 100 percent disabled veteran and they had no right to keep or touch him. He signed himself out of the hospital and got another fifth of gin to drink.

Being naïve, I thought that I had some special powers and had caused the accident by saying he would have one. I had to stop wishing or making statements of that nature because I was told it was the work of the devil.

My grandmother died in July 1967 from breast cancer, and I was devastated by the loss. She stayed with us briefly during her illness, and I had a lot of time to bond with her. During the summer months, I used to take a taxi cab to the Washington Hospital Center to feed her at lunchtime. My mother would go at the dinner hour, and sometimes I would go back with her. When the doctors said they couldn't do anything to prolong her life, my grandmother decided she wanted to go home. When she arrived home to die, she asked my grandfather to paint the house pink, green and white. I don't know what my other relatives thought, but I thought she had gone crazy. However, my grandfather honored her request and never once complained about it. Very soon after that, my grandmother died. I truly miss her. We had a special bond that no one could break. They say when a soul transitions another soul is on its way. In some ways it consoles me to think my grandmother may come back to us again as another baby in the family.

CHAPTER 15
The Abortion

I had heard that I had an older brother, and I found out for sure when he came home from the Navy to visit my mother. I couldn't believe it was really true, but he looked just like her. He came to the house and asked my mother if he could take me to the Howard Theater to see James Brown and the Famous Flames. When I got back from the show, I could move my feet and do a split just like James Brown. I enjoyed the show and I especially enjoyed that time with my older brother. Phillip got married right after that visit.

Phillip and his family visited us at times, but my stepfather had a big fight with him on one of those visits. From then on my brother preferred to come and get me to visit with his kids every now and then. I enjoyed spending my time with him and my sister-in-law, Paula. They had three children and Paula was pregnant with another one. Their second child, LaValda, was brain damaged from a difficult forcep delivery. Shortly after the death of my grandmother, Paula gave birth to a beautiful little girl. I asked her if she would name her after me, but she didn't like the name Thomasine, so she named her Thelma Cindy. We all called her Cindy. She was the prettiest child Phillip and Paula had. Little did I know that Paula and I were pregnant at the same time during her last pregnancy.

In February 1968, when I was 17, my mother and I found out that I was three months pregnant by Simon Benton. My mother had been telling me she was going to take me to get some birth control pills for my birthday. She became pregnant with Phillip when she was 17 and she didn't want that to happen to me. I guess she forgot because she was grieving over the death of my grandmother. When she took me to see our family doctor, he decided I needed a blood test, and the results showed that I was pregnant. My mother was upset to say the least. She asked the doctor if he knew of someone who could do an abortion, or if he could do one. He told her he couldn't because it was illegal.

The minute my mother got home she called Bertha Benton, and

they discussed the situation. The next thing I knew, I was taken to see an old white lady in someone's private home. The lady performed an illegal abortion on me. It was done on a Friday, and that Saturday, I went for a long walk because I was told exercise would hurry the process. On Sunday morning around 7:00 a.m., I started having pains in my abdomen.

I could not scream out from the pain because my stepfather would have heard me. He had already warned me that if I got pregnant, I could not stay there. As far as I know, my mother never told him I was pregnant. The pains got worse with time. I remember crawling around on the bathroom floor trying to keep from making any noise. My stepfather was suffering from a hangover, and I knew he couldn't hear me because he was snoring quite loudly in the other room. He was oblivious to what was happening in his own house. Around 9:00 a.m., I sat on the toilet and out came this bloody mass. My mother cut the cord and flushed the child down the toilet. I was sick and in pain for a long time. Eventually, I had to return to our family doctor, who prescribed some pills to relieve severe blood clotting.

In the meantime, Simon was getting ready to go into the Army. I always thought that was his way of getting away from me. We continued to see each other before he left, but I had birth control pills by then. Simon asked me if I would wait for him until he got out of the service. I agreed, but I was very depressed over the abortion. No one asked me what I wanted or how I felt about what had happened. All the decisions were made for me. I guess I really didn't have any say in the matter. I felt guilty for years after that ordeal and had to work with a psychiatrist to overcome the trauma.

In September 1968, I worked part-time at my old elementary school as a teacher's aide. That also kept me from Aunt Claire's house and out of trouble for a while. When Simon came back home after basic training, I was glad to see him. He asked me to marry him and we went to pick out a ring. We selected a nice sized diamond with a gold mounting and a gold band. He paid $125.00 for the whole set. I went to my new job at the school with a very beautiful ring on my finger. My mother made us promise that we would not get married before he got out of the service. She told him "In six months Thomasine will forget all about you." She was right. I don't think it even took six months. Deep down, I resented Simon for going into the service and for expecting me to have the abortion. I was in pain from what happened, but no one ever asked me how I felt. My mother, Simon, and Bertha Benton made the decision for me. I'm glad I did not have the child because I truly believe I would not have been a good mother. I believe I would have been a bad parent because of all of the abuse I experienced by different men and women.

CHAPTER 16
Life after School

I transferred from Roosevelt High School to Burdick Vocational High School. Because I didn't find the courses at Burdick to be college preparatory, I decided to transfer back to Roosevelt. When I arrived there in September 1967, school officials informed me that I had enough credits to graduate before my class of 1969. I asked for my diploma to be dated June 1968, but the principal's decision was to let me work under a special program for the under-privileged and give me my diploma with the class of 1969. So in June 1969, I was at work instead of at the graduation ceremony. That suited me just fine.

I was glad my mother did not get to see me walk across the stage at graduation. I was still resentful that she had missed my elementary school graduation because she was laid up in bed from a beating. I remember being devastated that she was not there for me, and I made a promise to myself that if I ever graduated from high school, she wouldn't see me walk across the stage. That's what I told myself at the time, but I was really trying to hide my fear that I would be disappointed by her a second time.

The District Government

In September 1968, I started working in the superintendent's office as a secretary's assistant for the D.C. Jail. The superintendent was nice, but stern. I remember that there was a firm rule that we could not talk to the trustees. The trustees were the inmates who were allowed to work in different offices. Employees were not allowed to mingle with any ex-offenders or parolees. I obeyed those rules because I didn't want to lose my first government job.

Aunt Claire knew several officers at the building where I worked. The superintendent's office had a wall of glass windows and from time to time, I would see officers come down the hall and stare inside. It was like they were looking for someone in particular. One day Aunt Claire called me and asked if I knew an officer Crowe. I said I knew his name from the mailroom, but I had never seen him in person. Well two days later, officer Crowe was in my office staring at me like I was a piece of meat. Then two or three days later, Lt. Woodward came to see me. I called my aunt and asked her what was going on. She said those guys were friends of hers, and she told them I was a good working girl. I had never seen them at my aunt's house.

Simon came back home on leave, and at first I was happy to see him. He soon got on my last nerve. It was clear that whatever we had in common was gone. I didn't tell him anything. I pretended everything was okay, but I was so glad when his two weeks were up. I realize now that I was angry with him for what happened and that is why I wanted to end the relationship.

At my job, I met just about all of the dayshift officers. One in particular, officer Buck Wilson, caught my eye. He told me he was 36 and had never been married. One day he told me his car had been stolen, and that he needed a ride. I told him he could get a ride with me if he showed me how to get to Andrews Air Force Base in Maryland. He agreed and we started talking. He asked me why I was going to Andrews. I told him I wanted to apply for a part-time job as a waitress. He told me that was no place for a young lady like me to be in. Later on during the week he asked me if I would have dinner with him. Of course, I had to drive because his car had been stolen from a government parking lot. I later found out from another officer that his car had not been stolen; it had been repossessed.

Buck and I went to a lot of parties and often visited some of his friends. We also started staying at a hotel in the city on the weekends. We registered as Mr. and Mrs. Wilson. When I look back on the situation, I realize that it was very dumb to register as a married couple because two married people would not need to stay in a motel.

Buck was a real "L-7," meaning a big square. He didn't know anything about a blowjob or any of the kinky stuff I knew. I felt I needed to pretend that I didn't know anything about sex when I was with him. Anyway, he only knew two ways of fucking, either me on top, or him on top, and he knew absolutely nothing about foreplay.

Aunt Claire had a boyfriend who had robbed a bank and had also been busted for selling drugs. When he was sentenced to do five years, she asked me if I wanted to move into his apartment, which was located in D.C. I was so determined to leave home by the age of 18 that I moved in and continued to pay the rent for four months. That was the agreement between my aunt and myself. I thought after paying the rent on time for those four months, I had proven that I could be responsible, so I applied for the apartment with the management office and I was approved. Since I was already in the apartment, the only thing I had to do was have the electricity, gas, and telephone turned on in my name. Apparently the management company had not checked on my references. When they eventually called my mother's house for a reference, someone told them that I was not responsible, and that I didn't even have a job. After that, they didn't even call the jail to see if I was working there. They just called me at the apartment and told me that I had to move out immediately. I was very shocked and hurt. I knew that the only person who would do something like that was my stepfather.

I didn't know what else to do, so I called Buck and asked him if he would apply for the apartment in his name. He did and was approved immediately. Of course, he wanted keys. He never would have been given a key if I had been able to rent on my own, and I truly believe life for me would have been much different. Years later I found out that it was my mother and not my stepfather who had given me the bad reference. She didn't want me to move away from home.

In September 1969, my job for the District government was coming to an end. I had one of those positions that could not exceed one year. The superintendent's office transferred me to the finance office because they needed someone in that office to help the chief finance officer. The chief finance officer asked for an extension for me right away. He was very happy with my work and I liked working there because it was challenging. The program that I was in was hiring other students and disabled veterans. One young man, Allan Brown, came to work in the finance office too. After only three or four months he confided in me that he needed to marry his girlfriend because she was pregnant, but he didn't have much money. I felt sorry for him and offered to sell him a real nice set of wedding rings. I sold the set Simon gave me to Allan for $150.00. He was glad to get it and they married soon after he bought the rings.

In October 1969, Buck and I started living together in that one bedroom apartment. Buck was a hard worker and a heavy drinker. He liked the same type of music I liked. Pain music, as Dr. Welsing calls it.

CHAPTER 17
My Escape From Home

Because the wheels of government move so slowly, I thought my job in the District government would never be extended, so, one Sunday after church, I asked my pastor if he needed a secretary. He hired me two weeks later. I found that working in a church office was very different from working at my other job. It was fun. I was surprised that church people were so lively. Quite a few of them appeared to be rather fond of alcohol, though they generally tried to conduct themselves appropriately.

Since I had worked on that one job in the District government, I thought I knew everything there was to know about being a secretary. I was wrong. I was one of the pastor's favorite people at that time, but unlike me, he was a perfectionist with a capital P. I had to retype many of his letters over and over until I got them right. My biggest problem was centering a letter in the middle of the page.

Around February of 1970, at age 19, I started falling asleep every day from 12:30 to 2:00 p.m. I told Buck that there was something wrong with me because I was always so sleepy. He told me to quit the job, come home, and keep the apartment clean. I went to my pastor and told him that I had to quit and he said, "I'm glad you came to me before I had to fire you." We hugged and I left that Friday, relieved that we had ended on a happy note.

Things went well for a while, but I suspected Buck was seeing someone else. When I confronted him with it, he became very defensive. Then, I actually caught him on the phone with the person and interrupted the conversation. That's when he started beating me. He hit me on my head, on the sides of my body, and other areas where the bruises wouldn't show. He apologized the next day and promised never to hit me again. He also told me I was the only person he had ever hit, and he didn't understand why he was beating me. I accepted his apology and hoped things would get better. In reality, I had gone from one abusive situation to another by falling in love with Buck.

CHAPTER 18
Pregnant Again

I made an appointment to see a gynecologist because I had started throwing up every morning and sometimes in the evenings. My doctor told me that I was three months pregnant. Buck seemed to be happy at first, but as time went on, he began to sing along with a particular song that came on the radio every morning around 7:00 a.m. The song was called, "Mama's Baby, Daddy's Maybe." While singing, he would rub my stomach. I can't explain the pain and rage I felt when he rubbed my stomach. It hurt that Buck would be so nasty.

Around that same time, I found out Buck was calling his long-time girlfriend, Florence Stuart. Both Buck and Florence had gone to Howard University together and were college sweethearts. All of their friends called her the Ram and him the Bull, and they all thought that the two love birds would get married after graduation. Why they didn't marry always puzzled me, because, from all accounts, they were a perfect couple. But we had become a couple and the more he continued the relationship with her the angrier I got. I experienced a jealousy and rage I had never experienced before in my life when I learned that he had contacted and visited her.

I asked Buck when we were going to get married since I was pregnant. He would give me a date, and when that date arrived he would say, "I'm working overtime." He did get the marriage license and kept it almost a year before we actually got married.

Buck and I got into a major physical fight in April of 1970 when I was approximately four months pregnant. After that beating, I couldn't move for two days. I felt Buck didn't care about me or his unborn child.

We had a joint bank account with American Security and Trust with approximately $500.00 in the account. I went to the bank and removed all but $50.00 and then I went to Aunt Claire and asked her if she knew someone who would perform an abortion. She did. She hooked me up with some black guy who performed illegal abortions. On April

30, I met the man in a vacant house somewhere in D.C. By this time, I was very close to being five months pregnant. This guy didn't even have a bed or a blanket for me to lie on, so I had to lie on the hardwood floor. The minute he inserted a red tube into my vagina, I knew I had made a mistake by coming to this guy instead of trying to find someone who was more professional. I again ignored my intuition.

After the procedure was over, I went to my aunt's house to rest. She offered me one of the bedrooms in her basement, and I settled in for the night. The next day, I called my mother to let her know what I had done. She was very surprised at my decision. The whole time I was there, she kept calling to check on me and Aunt Claire would answer the phone. On the third day, my water broke and my mother came over to see how I was getting along. When she arrived, she and Aunt Claire got into an argument because my mother wanted my aunt to help me instead of attending to her business. Aunt Claire said that she couldn't make any money running back and forth looking after me.

In the meantime, the pain was much worse than before. The child came sometime late in the night. My aunt and my mother were there with me and said the baby was a boy. They got rid of it for me. I never knew what they did with it, which was just as well because I intended to leave it outside the door to Buck's apartment. I was just that angry over his relationship with Florence and his lack of support during my pregnancy.

Knocking At Death's Door

After the birth, instead of getting better I got worse. I had a temperature of 103 and felt like I had the flu. My mother called me and didn't like the way I sounded, so she came over to my aunt's to check on me. After Aunt Claire said she didn't have time to baby-sit me and try to sell pussy too, my mother took me to my doctor's office, and he immediately had me admitted to the Washington Hospital Center. But before checking me into the hospital, he asked for $210.00, upfront. He wanted me to sit in the hospital lobby and wait for my mother to go get the money. I ended up going along for the ride with my mother because the cool air felt so good to my face.

The hospital asked for an insurance card, and I told them that I didn't have it with me but I would have my mother bring it back. They admitted me on that promise, and I knew that I would have to get Buck's Blue Cross/Blue Shield card as soon as possible. When we were out of hearing range of the admission staff, I told my mother to find Buck as fast as she could. The doctors examined me and placed me on the critical list. I had no idea that I was near death. My blood pressure was extremely high, and I was dying because the afterbirth had not expelled itself and had caused a terrible infection that was spreading throughout my body. Buck finally called me and said, "You made your bed hard and now lay in it." The next day he came to the hospital to visit me for a short time, and he gave the hospital the necessary insurance information. After five days, I was discharged.

During my stay, the doctor told Buck that he had no idea why I went from being a happy mother-to-be to one desperate enough to see a butcher. He said that he could have turned us all in to the police because the abortion was illegal. To make matters worse, the abortion was incomplete, and I almost lost my life. After talking to the doctor, Buck walked into my room crying like a baby. I was discharged and given a very strong antibiotic for the infection. I was told to report back to the doctor within two weeks. After the two weeks, I was in much better shape, but still weak. I had no job and really nowhere else to go, so I stayed with Buck.

Buck went to the bank sometime while I was in the hospital to deposit some money into our joint savings account. Before the transaction took place, he asked the teller to give him his balance. The teller told him it was $50.00. He said, "I believe you are mistaken. You have your decimal point in the wrong place." The teller said, "No your wife came in and withdrew $450.00." Buck never let me forget that I took the money out. He also wanted to know why I had the abortion, but I had a hard time putting my feelings into words, and I never answered him. I was also confused about what had happened. So, I said nothing, and he believed whatever he wanted to believe. I didn't try to defend myself. There again, I felt pain, shame, and guilt.

CHAPTER 19
Buck's Family

Buck's mother, Mrs. Lucille Wilson, died at the end of June 1970. She was a live-in maid in New York City, and her employer found her. She had died in her sleep. Later we found out she had died from complications of diabetes. I had never met her formally, but had spoken to her many times over the phone. She thought the sun rose and set on Buck. As she would say, "He is my baby."

After getting the news about his mother, Buck and I hopped a train to New York. Percy, Buck's younger brother, met us at the station. I was totally shocked to find out that Buck had a brother. Percy was married to Sandra and they had a son, Keith, who was about 18 months old. Buck and Percy made the arrangements for Mrs. Wilson to be viewed at a funeral home in New York. Then her body was taken by train to Lexington, Kentucky, for a small service and interment.

When I was pregnant, Buck had hounded me that any baby I had had better be light-skinned because his mother was light-skinned. He said if the baby wasn't light, bright and damn near white, it was not his. Well, I was extremely surprised when I finally saw Mrs. Lucille Wilson. She was very dark skinned. I had been afraid the whole time I was pregnant because I was sure the baby would come out looking as jet black as my grandfather and Buck would never believe that the baby was his. I made a promise to myself never to get pregnant again because I knew it would be a disaster. If the father was not going to be there to support the child financially and emotionally and be a true father to the child, I was not going to have a baby for anyone. I was not going to allow my child to be raised as I had been.

On the trip home from New York, Buck told me he had several sisters and brothers. It was hard to believe that they did not show up at their own mother's funeral. It seemed that her employer thought more of her than her own children.

We then hopped another train at Union Station in D.C. It took twelve hours to get to Lexington, Kentucky. The ride had been long, and the train was extremely cold because the air conditioner was turned up real high. I wore a really thin dress and I thought I would freeze my butt off, but it never occurred to me to ask for a blanket.

When we arrived in Kentucky, C.C., the oldest child of Aunt Belinda and Jack Chase, came to get the body. The Chase family owned the funeral home hired to finalize the arrangements. Percy and Sandra arrived before us, and the rest of the family was there as well. I finally met Buck's so-called brothers and sisters, along with Magdalene, Sara B., his uncles, C.C., Perry, and Buck's Aunt Mandy and her husband. I met his great aunts Sylvia, Wanda, and Katie, and Katie's husband McArthur Oldham. Buck finally made it clear that the brothers and sisters he had talked about were really his cousins who he considered brothers and sisters. They were a down-to-earth, fun-loving bunch of good people. I connected with them the very first day I got there.

I met a lot of Buck's friends, schoolmates, and teachers. They all thought the world of him. Little did they know that he believed in kicking ass first and taking names later.

After Mrs. Wilson was buried, we all ate and got a chance to know each other better. Everyone could tell that I was much younger than Buck, and they all thought we were married. Upon leaving Kentucky, after staying there a week, we all promised to keep in touch. A schoolmate of Buck's, Cathy Grant, and I remained friends even after our divorce.

CHAPTER 20
My Old Habit

After burying his mother, Buck and I came home and settled back into our routine. He went back to work, and I sat around the house. I started visiting Aunt Claire again around July 1970. Again, Buck and I got into a big fight over some woman he was dating, and I left for the 15th time. Every time I left I would vow never to return.

As was my pattern in those days, I went to Aunt Claire's house with no money and no job in sight. I started turning tricks and was again using my body to earn money. I had no respect for myself and no understanding of self love in those days.

There was a whole new set of men coming to see my aunt this time around, but some old johns like Timmy, Jeff, and Clifton were still coming around. Upon returning, I met two brothers, Joey and Jessie. Joey was 6' 5" and real skinny. Aunt Claire wanted him for herself. She told me that his dick hung down around his knees. I tried him out, but I couldn't handle it. He reminded me of Harold because he had a bald head, was real slim, and had a long dick.

Joey's brother was quiet and muscular, but he fucked you every which way but loose. Delores, their sister, was one of the many girls at my aunt's house, and she brought her brothers over for my aunt to meet. Delores was bisexual. She didn't care who she saw just as long as they had money.

I made a lot of money during that time while I was with Aunt Claire. By then, I'm sure her children, including her youngest daughter Linda, who was only 10, were aware of what I was doing. It was obvious that I was selling myself.

I was a witness to how sick some people really are in bed. There were a few johns who liked to engage in threesomes, like this white guy who wanted me and another girl to have sex with him. The girl was really nice and reminded me of the actress Pam Grier. I had never experienced anything like it, so I kind of played with the guy's penis while the other girl did all the work. That freaky fool wanted one of us to beat him with a belt while a candle was inserted in his butt. I did the beating; the other girl gave him a blowjob. The candle stayed in place on it's own. When the other girl started eating his butt, I thought I would faint from the sight. Believe me, he got his rocks off in a big way because the stuff shot all over the place. I never indulged in anything like that again.

Buck was working at a halfway house as a correctional treatment specialist under Ashford Cooper. He worked the evening shift, which gave him a lot of freedom to do as he pleased. There was an inmate there by the name of Tony. One day my car stopped running, and Tony came to my rescue. He gave me a jump and followed me to my aunt's house to make sure I got home safely. I invited him in for something cool to drink. He accepted and later that day we went to Rock Creek Park to talk. I told him that Buck and I were not really married and that I had decided to leave him alone because of his abuse. Tony and I connected, and he asked me out. Soon we were spending a lot of time together. I really enjoyed being with him, until I went to bed with him. Tony couldn't do anything; the thing was dead, but he was stuck on me. It seemed like I couldn't get rid of him no matter what I did.

My car started acting up again one week when Aunt Claire and I decided to go to Atlantic City for some rest and relaxation. Tony agreed to work on the car while I was gone and have it fixed by the time I returned. While I was away, he drove my car to the halfway house and told everyone he was dating me. He also told a few of the guys that he wanted to marry me. Word got back to Buck. When I arrived back at my aunt's house, my car had been stolen. Now who would want to steal an old 1966 Corvair in 1970? The car leaked oil and smelled to high heaven from gas and oil fumes. I immediately called Buck to see if he knew anything about the disappearance of the car. He said he didn't, and he wanted to help me find it. I replied "No thanks, but I will be calling the police as soon as I am finished talking to you." He begged me not to call the police. I called the police and made a report anyway. They found the car right around the corner from Aunt Claire's house.

Buck called me the next day or so and asked if I would go with him to a liquor store on Rt. 301 near Waysons Corner, and I agreed to go just for the ride. On our way, it was dark and cold and I started to wonder if this man was going to kill me and leave my body in the woods. Instead, he asked me if I had given any thought to getting married. I told him no; I had changed my mind. He told me Percy and Sandra were coming to D.C. to visit. He did not ask me to join them, but when they arrived, Percy called me at my aunt's house and asked me to join them for dinner at Blackie's House of Beef. I went out and purchased a very sexy black jump suit, shoes, and a new purse. The jumpsuit was made in such a way that I couldn't wear a bra with it, so my breasts were exposed a little, and the waist area was made of a see-through mesh material the color of my skin. It was very tastefully done. Although I sold my body, I never dressed like a street hooker. All of my clothes were very tasteful, and every hair on my head was always in place. I liked to look good.

When I entered the restaurant, everyone turned around and looked at me. Even Buck looked twice and made some kind of comment under his breath. Of course, Percy was glad to see me. He and I always got along. He drank a lot, but he didn't try to hit on me or anything. He had divided the savings bonds up from their mother's estate and brought Buck his half of the money. We all enjoyed each other's company so much that we decided to stay up half the night talking. When it was time for me to go, Buck asked me to stay the night in the same hotel as his brother and his sister-in-law, and I agreed.

When we finally got into bed, Buck started kissing me and crying and telling me how much he missed me. I realized I missed our life in the apartment. We made love like we had never made love before. He cried and I cried. He apologized and I apologized. The next morning, I went back to my aunt's to change and Buck and I took Percy and his wife sightseeing. They went home the next day, and Buck and I went our separate ways like nothing ever happened.

CHAPTER 21
The Marriage

A week or so after we spent the night together, Buck called me and asked me to come over to the apartment to see him. When I got there, he told me we were going to get married. I really didn't believe him. I thought he would get up the next morning and tell me he had to go to work. Instead, he had me go with him to pick out a new suit, shirt and tie, and a new pair of shoes. The next day he took me to Urgdon's, a very nice dress shop on F Street, where I found a white lace shirt dress. I found the perfect shoes at Hahn's shoe store and a cute little hat at Kahn's department store. Buck asked me to call Rev. Singleton to make arrangements for us to get married after church services on Sunday. I refused. I told him he would never make me look like a fool again. So, he called and made the arrangements.

I expected Buck to change his mind after we got to church, but he didn't. We were married 2:00 p.m. Sunday, September 6, 1970, at John Wesley A.M.E. Zion Methodist Church. I could hardly believe we went through with it. We went home, packed, and left for New York and stayed with Percy and Sandra for a couple of days.

The Family's Reaction

Now, I was the legal wife of Buck Wilson. When I told my stepfather, he just kept saying, "Shit, shit, shiiiiiiiiit. It won't last long enough for water to get hot." When I told my mother, she got all upset because I had gotten married at church in front of all her friends, and she was not there. I explained that I really didn't think Buck was going to go through with the marriage. I reminded her how many times he had promised me before and always had an excuse that he had to work. My mother ranted for years about me not inviting her, but she finally got over it.

Buck's Abusive Patterns

When Buck finally moved all of his things from his old girlfriend's apartment to our apartment, I found papers on his divorce from Cora Grass. Cora filed for the divorce on the grounds of mental and physical cruelty. I thought to myself when I read the grounds for their divorce, "Oh God what have I gotten myself into?" I also prayed for Buck and told God, "Now that I've got him, I don't know what in the hell to do with him." That's why they say, be careful for what you ask for. You just might get it.

Aunt Claire didn't care that I was married. She continued to call me to come and turn some more tricks. You know she had to feed those six children of hers. I didn't refuse because deep down I was afraid she would tell Buck what I was really doing at her house. He knew what she was doing, but he never thought I was participating in her business. So, out of fear, I continued to see guys during the day and was home in time to fix Buck's dinner at night.

Buck was still seeing other women. They would even call the house and ask for him, and if I asked who they were, they would say, "Tell him it's a friend." When I confronted him with this, he would beat me and tell me to stop getting into his business.

As time went on, I began to worry. I was turning tricks more and more. I became afraid that one day one of Buck's friends would come to my aunt's house or maybe one day my own father would walk through those doors. How was I to know what type of person my father was? Every person in my life was drinking, gambling, buying pussy, and doing whatever. I really thought that was the norm. I could have had intercourse with him and not known it was my father. I started to pray and ask the Lord to take away the desire to make money in that manner. I prayed day and night. I had heard it said that you go to your "closet" and Jesus would never reveal your sins. I literally did just that. I told the Lord this was our project. It was He and I alone. I made up my mind that if my aunt called, I would turn her down. It didn't always work that way though. Sometimes, I wanted a new dress, or I needed the companionship of a man and the temptation was hard to resist.

I started to feel more and more insecure. Buck was busy working overtime, drinking, and cutting out on me. He didn't have the time or the energy to take care of my needs mentally or physically. I started to worry that he didn't really love me. There were times I would cry for his attention. I even cried at times because Buck would refuse to have sex with me. I guess that was because he was too tired. Afterall, he was 18 years my senior.

The Turning Point

I went to my closet, as the Bible states, and took my burdens to the Lord. I found myself on my knees every morning and every night I prayed in silence in my bed. I asked the Lord to please give me the strength. I knew that I was worrying the Lord to death, but I didn't care. We had to work this out. I was fighting a vicious cycle of saying no and returning to my old pattern a week later. I'd be back seeing Mr. Austin and then back on my knees asking for forgiveness and strength.

I tried having an affair, but the guilt was too overwhelming for me. I couldn't do it anymore. There were plenty of men who wanted to take me out, but they all worked with me, and they were all married. After two affairs with different men, I stopped. None of the affairs ever lasted more than a month and none of them ever satisfied the emotional need to be loved that I had inside of me.

CHAPTER 22
The Homicide

Aunt Claire was still calling me to come back, and I was still saying no. Then she stopped calling for a while because she had a new boyfriend. His name was Pete. He had a construction company and was making big money. By my aunt's standards, he was rich. They were dating a long time when she suspected that Pete was seeing someone else. To add insult to injury, she'd heard that he was dating a white chick. She became possessed with jealousy. One night he invited a few people to a small party he was having at his house, but she was not invited. She found out about the party and went to his house very late. When she got there, she asked Pete to take a ride with her and he agreed. He ended up dead with a gunshot wound to his upper body. The newspapers said my aunt shot him and drove him around for two to four hours before taking him to an area hospital. He was pronounced dead upon arrival at the hospital. She was taken to the Women's Detention Center and was arraigned the following Monday.

Aunt Claire called me to ask if I knew a "Perry Mason lawyer." I told her I didn't. Due to the investigation into the murder, she had to stop the activities in her house. She already had a long record, which included petty larceny, selling liquor, and the attempted murder of her first husband. Now, she was charged with murder in the first degree, so she knew it was best that she lay low. She later told me she had an attorney by the name of George McGuire. We never discussed the case, and she eventually got off on self-defense.

After that long ordeal, Aunt Claire started having heart problems, and she was told she didn't have long to live. If I remember correctly, she was told she had a leaking heart valve. She called me over to her house and told me that she wanted to give me something special since I was her only niece. She gave me her diamond ring. It was beautiful, and I had always admired it. I never thought I would get the prettiest ring she had. She gave all of her daughters a gift of either a diamond ring or a mink coat. She went out and brought Pearl, her oldest daughter, a full-length mink coat. Pearl looked wonderful in that coat and wore it everywhere.

By this time, life at my aunt's house was slow. The men only stopped by to say hello. Juanita and Wanda, the two other madams in the area, had been raided, so business was real slow. The police were watching my aunt, and although she had gotten away with killing Pete, they still wanted to get her on something.

CHAPTER 23
Meeting My Father

In February of 1972, when I was 21, my mother and I went to a "nip and sip." The nip and sips were dances that took the place of cabarets. People sipped wine and ate cheese and other finger food and danced to a little jazz. My mother's cousin, Melinda, was there. She told my mother I looked just like Lawrence, my father. She asked me if I had ever met him and I told her no. Melinda looked at my mother and told her that she was wrong for not introducing me to him. On the way home, I begged my mother to get in touch with my father. I had been longing to meet him for years. The next morning, I called my mother and asked her again. She finally agreed to call him.

After my mother got in touch with my father, she called me back and said he would be calling me from work. She gave me his work number just in case he didn't call me. I waited by the phone for two days like I was expecting the president of United States to call. He never called, so I called him. A gentleman answered the phone saying, "United States Conference of Mayors." It was my father. When I realized who I was talking to, I became very nervous and my stomach was in knots. I asked him if we could meet for lunch at some time, and he agreed to pick me up two days later.

The day I met my father, I wore a red velvet dress with off black stockings and black high heels. He was dressed in a very nice suit and tie. He arrived on time driving a big four-door Cadillac. There were 12 long-stem yellow roses for me on the backseat of his car. We went to the Ritz Carlton Hotel on 16th Street for their lunch buffet. It was very elegant with linen tablecloths and formal place settings. Neither of us ate because we were too excited. We talked for hours. He said he wished he could have been a part of my life. It was what I needed to hear from him.

My father took me home, and I took the roses in and put them in a vase. I remember that those roses lasted a week or more. They were so beautiful. I called everyone I could think of and told them about meeting my real father. When Buck got home, I told him, and he seemed to be very happy for me. Everyone thought it was a fairy tale type story.

The next day my father called and asked me if he could bring his wife over to see me. I agreed and made dinner for them. I ordered a cake from Clements, my favorite bakery. The cake read Happy St. Patrick's Day. It was March 17th. My father's wife, Zelma, was very quiet and very cautious. We all ate dinner in somewhat of a guarded and uneasy way. I was not much of a cook then. I can imagine the food was just edible.

Two or three days went by and I received a call from Daddy asking if he and Zelma could come by. I asked Buck and they were there within 10 minutes. They brought some cold cuts from a deli not far from our apartment. This time they got a chance to meet my husband. They were shocked to find out he was much older than me. They were pleasant, but you could see their disapproval. When my father got me alone, he asked me, "Where did you get such an old man for a husband?" I told him that I liked older men. He told me if he had a hand in raising me, I would have never married an old man. As he stated, I would have gone to college and married someone closer to my own age and with money.

The next Sunday, they took me to visit Zelma's relatives in Indian Head, Maryland. I met her mother and several brothers, sisters, nieces, and nephews. My father never really introduced me. He just asked all of them who they thought I looked like. Zelma and Daddy were playing a game with her family members. It was a game I really didn't like. All of them responded that I could be Lawrence's sister. That is when both Zelma and Lawrence told them I was his long-lost daughter. They were all surprised, but accepted me as a part of the Wren family. I was a real likable person back then and able to hide the things in my life that would make others uncomfortable.

The next weekend, I was to meet my grandfather, his wife, and Aunt Della and her family. I ended up falling right into their game playing again. They would say, "Who do you think this is?" They all looked puzzled, all except my father's stepmother. She knew right away. She could run her mouth from the time you got there until you left without you saying a word. She was kind enough to ask me how my mother was right in front of my father and Zelma. Aunt Della and her husband were real quiet and kind people, but it was as if they all did not know what to say. I believed they were all uncomfortable with meeting me. Charlene, Aunt Della's daughter, was glad to have a cousin on her mother's side of the family. Her birthday is the day after mine and we celebrated together for years. Charlene and I are the only grandchildren on my father's side of the family.

Approximately two months later, Charlene and her husband Allen came to visit my father and Zelma. Buck and I went over there so that I could introduce them to my husband. I didn't know it at the time but Charlene and Allen were having problems of their own, and she was planning to leave him. He was struggling with drug addiction, and he was physically abusive. I didn't hear from Charlene again until she had divorced Allen.

While visiting my father and Zelma one Sunday, he asked me to hand him a cookie container. When I picked it up, I noticed the silver detailing and porcelain on the inside. I asked him where he got the cookie jar and he told me that an old lady gave it to him with a pitcher to match. I told him that I had seen the matching pitcher to it and that my mother had just given it to Mama M, who lived next door to us. I explained that Mama M used to take care of me after school. My father told me he would do just about anything to get that pitcher back, so I went to see Mama M that week and told her the story. She already knew the story of how I met my father, and she thought it was wonderful. I made arrangements for him to meet Mama M and Zepora. He took Mama M an old kerosene lantern, and she gave him the pitcher. They talked for at least an hour about antiques. Mama M's house was full of antiques, which I truly believe were my father's first love.

My father and Zelma took Buck and me to Williamsburg, Virginia, for a weekend trip. We stayed at the Williamsburg Inn. The inn had lots of antiques and was a very nice place. We walked around looking in the many shops and had wonderful meals in the inn's restaurant. I remember there weren't any televisions in the rooms, and Buck was very bored because he could not drink or look at a football game as he normally did on the weekends. I would have preferred to go with Daddy and Zelma without Buck because he complained about everything the entire weekend and tainted the specialness of my time with my father.

There were times when my father questioned me about my upbringing. He would say he thought my mother did a good job of raising me. At other times, he said he felt he could have made my life different if he had raised me. He thought I should have gone to college. I believe he was insecure because another man raised me instead of him. He came right out and asked me if he and my stepfather were sick at the same time, who would I go to first. I told him that I would have to see about my stepfather because I grew up with him. I knew I had said the wrong thing, but I was frustrated because I felt I was always being tested by my father.

Zelma was beginning to become very jealous of my new relationship with my father. Daddy gave me some money for an Easter outfit so I could go to church with him. When Zelma found out that he gave me some money, she went out and purchased an outfit too.

One evening my father asked me if I would help him work in his office. He was responsible for getting the weekly Congressional Report out. I agreed, and Zelma, Daddy, and I went to his office. Zelma wouldn't work. She just sat in a chair and cried the whole evening. I asked Daddy what he thought the problem was and he said she was going through the change. I knew there was something more to it, but when I asked Zelma, she never replied. Later on that night Zelma sat Buck, Daddy, and me down at my house and told us how she really felt about her husband taking up so much time with me. She was furious about it. She was in tears the entire time she was trying to explain how she felt. Zelma said she would have been able to accept me if I had come into their lives at an earlier age, like ten years old. She asked my husband what I wanted from her and Daddy. Buck was very honest for once in his life and told her I only wanted to meet my father and have a father-daughter relationship with him. Zelma came right out and asked if I wanted money. Buck and I both said no. Buck and I went to bed that night worried about Zelma and feeling sorry for her because of what she was going through. I had always believed she poisoned my father against me. Years later, I found that not to be true.

My father and I had a private conversation later that week. I asked him not to buy me anything or mention me to Zelma for a while. I asked him to give Zelma some TLC. My father said he wanted to change his will after meeting me, and I told him not to mention it to her for a while because she would think I put him up to it. I also told him I would not come over for a while, and I even suggested that we meet for lunch without her. That agreement only lasted for two weeks. My father and I could not stay away from each other. We were on the phone all the time. We were too much alike.

CHAPTER 24
Going Back to Work

Daddy thought it was awful that I didn't work. He told me that every woman needed to work, so he called me everyday to see when I was going to look for a job. I returned to the previous agency in October 1971, and resumed working for the superintendent's office, but this time the superintendent was a very new person on the job. Sonya Green was his personal secretary. After working in that office for a year, I was promoted to GS-4.

Later, I applied for a job in another division. The old superintendent had been promoted to deputy director. Blair Woodstock was his secretary and been for years. When Blair found out that I was working three floors below her office, she insisted that we have lunch every other day.

Blair had been my first supervisor when I worked there back in 1967. When the director's secretary went on vacation, Blair asked me if I wanted to sit in for her. I agreed and, the next thing I knew, I was sitting in the director's office for three weeks. He was so impressed with me that he created a job in that office just for me.

I was there almost a year when something horrible happened. I was accused of doing something I didn't do and I was devastated because I had worked hard to prove myself. I was the new kid on the block, so to say. I was just beginning to work with people I thought were on a higher scale, and I was feeling good about my performance, but someone started a rumor that I had called Mrs. Goldsmith and told her that her husband was having an affair. The funny thing was that I only saw Mr. Goldsmith in the mornings when the director had his staff meetings with all the heads of the different departments. No one ever asked me if I had made the call, but before I knew it I was being transferred to a different job.

About three days before I was to leave, a Mrs. Goldsmith called to speak to the director and I took advantage of the opportunity to clear my name. I asked her if she was the wife of Mr. Goldsmith who worked in the office. When she answered yes, I told her what I had been accused of doing. She admitted that someone had called her, but she knew it was not me because of the tone of my voice and my mannerisms. I asked her to please let the director know she had spoken with me because they were sending me to another job. She promised she would, but I don't know if she ever did.

I was so nervous and preoccupied with all that was going on that I fell down a few steps that same day. I had to take a few days off to recuperate, and had time to think about what had happened and how it could have happened to me. I spoke to my friend Morris, who knew the ins and outs of the director's office. Morris told me that Mr. Goldsmith was seeing two women, and I was being used as the "fall guy." One of the women was an employee in my division and the other one was an employee from one of our regional offices. His advice was for me to call the director and let him know that I had some information that he needed to know about. In so many words, to tell what I knew. He quoted the regulations on employees having affairs with fellow co-workers, and he also asked me if I knew a congressman who would see me immediately in case the director wouldn't see me. I believe Morris was concerned that the director would try to create trumped-up charges against me, and it would be my word against his. I remembered the first person I prostituted myself to, who was a congressman, and I called his office and made an appointment for Monday, May 13, at 2:00 p.m. Then I called the director and he agreed to see me immediately.

I told the director all that I knew. By that time, I knew the two ladies and the other male employees involved in the scandal. I also told him that I knew that he knew about the situation, but refused to take any action against the employees. To conclude, I told him that I had an appointment with a friend who was a congressman, and if he did not do as I asked, I would be seeing him immediately. I know now that I really could have used the situation to my advantage, but all I asked for was my old job. I also promised him that I would remain silent if they left me alone and allowed my husband and me to receive any and all promotions on the merits of our work. He thought that was a fair deal and asked me to wait a week or two. Sure enough, I received a letter to report back to my old division. In the letter, the director thanked me for the wonderful job I had done in his office.

Buck was shocked when I told him what had happened. He said that, if he had heard that I had called Mrs. Goldsmith, he would have thought that I did it because I was obsessed with people cheating on each other. I made it clear that I didn't care about other people. I only wanted him to stop cheating on me.

After that incident, the employees in my unit who had heard the story had nothing to do with me. For years, I looked the woman in the eyes who had actually called Mrs. Goldsmith. I knew who she was, and I wanted to whip her ass for using my name, but I was afraid I would lose my good government job.

CHAPTER 25
Buck's Struggle with Alcoholism

In June of 1972, Buck passed out in one of the guard towers from an unknown diabetic condition. Not waiting for the paramedics to arrive, his fellow co-workers removed him from the tower down the very narrow stairway and somehow tore a ligament in his shoulder. He had surgery and lots of physical therapy and was unable to work for 18 months. Back then, when you applied for compensation, it took several weeks for the paperwork to get processed and then you had to wait for the check. With my half of the income tax return, which I had put in my savings account, and my paychecks, I managed to keep the household going. During this time, the doctors diagnosed Buck as an alcoholic. This was not news to me. I suspected that he was an alcoholic because he drank constantly. What was different about Buck compared to other alcoholics I knew, was that he could not get up and go to work on a regular basis. The others worked every day unless they had a bad hangover.

Buck had reached a point in his life where he could no longer drink a quart of scotch a day. His mind told him he could, but his body said no. Someone suggested that he go to Alcoholics Anonymous and that I go to Al-Anon, a group for the families of alcoholics. When I first attended the meetings, I had very little to say. All of the stories sounded so familiar. I started working the 12-step program and was doing pretty well. After attending the meetings for over six months, my sponsor asked me if I would speak to the group. I agreed and spoke about love with detachment. My sponsor was very proud of me because I was the youngest in the group.

On the night I spoke to the group, I made the mistake of reading the entire speech to Buck and showing him all of my background information. Well, after I finished, I got an ass beating I will never forget, and I didn't understand why it happened until after I spoke to my sponsor. She told me that my spouse was jealous because I was working the program better than he was. She told me to never repeat what I said or heard in the meetings. Sometimes the alcoholic is not ready to hear the truth, especially from his wife or another member of his family. After talking to my sponsor, I never discussed anything about the meetings with my husband.

I later learned that Buck was actively drinking during the times he should have been in his meetings, and he was seeing another woman. The meetings usually started at 8:00 p.m. and ended by 9:00 p.m. I would sometimes get into conversations with other members afterwards, but I was always home by 10:00 p.m. Buck was beginning to come home at 12:30 or 1:00 a.m. When I asked him why he was getting home so late, he would reply that the group would go to a coffee house to talk after the meetings. Buck did not drink coffee. Later on I found out that he was dating a woman who worked on the mid-night shift at the Public Hospital. He would leave his meeting at 9:00 p.m. and go to her house and stay with her until it was time to take her to work. Then he would come home and sleep with me until it was time to take me to work. After he dropped me off, he would take her back to her house.

It took me a while to figure it out. It didn't make sense for him to drive me to work when I was perfectly capable of driving myself. He was using the time after he left me to stay with her. He was working around my schedule so I wouldn't find out about his affair, but I eventually found photographs of his girlfriend taken in the park and nude photos of her taken in her house. One day on my way home in Buck's car, I stopped at a stop sign and while looking in the rear view mirror, I saw him two or three cars behind me. He was driving my Vega and there was someone else in the car with him. Because of the distance between the two cars, I couldn't see who was with him. To be certain that I was not mistaken, I sat there long enough to see the woman pull her ponytail around to her shoulder. Yes, she was light, bright and damn near white. She was what you called a 500 watt bulb red bone.

Although the signs were always apparent, until that day I had never actually seen him with another woman. I drove home slowly. Extremely upset, I went inside, sat in the recliner, and waited for Buck. Approximately 15 minutes after I got home, he showed up in a very good mood. He strolled in and asked me to go with him to Landover Mall to help him pick out a shirt, and he even offered to buy me anything I wanted. While Nancy Wilson's song "Guess Who I Saw Today" played in the background, I slowly looked him in the eyes and asked him, "Who was that woman in my fucking car?" He tried to tell me that it was no woman; it was Dick Smith. Buck was such a good liar that he almost had me convinced that I had seen a man. For a moment, I wondered if it really could have been a man with Buck, then I remembered the ponytail and said, "I guess Dick Smith has a ponytail." He eventually admitted it was the woman from the hospital, and said that they were arguing about whether or not he should pay for some work she needed done on her house. That's why he didn't notice me ahead of him in his car.

Buck told me he needed some time to think about things, and he started packing his clothes to go away for the weekend. At that point in time, I didn't care where he went, just as long as he got out of my face. Then I remembered that my father was taking us to visit my grandparents because they wanted to meet him. I asked if he would go so that my father wouldn't know we were having problems. He refused.

Buck ended up going to a hotel in the area and while he was gone, I found his phone book and called the woman. She was very surprised to hear me tell her she could have him. I said that I no longer wanted an alcoholic who never took a bath and only worked six months out of the year. I told her I had to beg his friends to come and literally put him in the tub and beg him to go get dried out. I also told her I was sick of finding the psychiatrists for his treatments and I was tired of feeling like I was the bad guy. I knew I didn't make him drink. He drank because he loved the taste of the alcohol.

By the time I finished talking to the woman, she was apologizing to me for contributing to my many heartaches. I let her know that she was not the only one he was fooling around with. She was one of many, and when he was caught, he would get drunk and confess it all to me. She promised never to call my house again. I told her I really didn't care what the fuck she did because I was finished with the situation.

The next day my father called ready to go to see my grandparents. I met him at his house and rode to Virginia with them. I tried to have fun, but everyone could tell something was wrong. I never mentioned the problem, but sensing that Buck was the problem, my father pulled me to the side and told me not to worry because he was a man who drank and needed the company of other alcoholics.

Buck came home drunk sometime the following Monday. As was his pattern, he stayed drunk for four months. I moved to the sofa in the living room and pushed all the windows up to keep the stench out. I waited approximately four weeks and then took an adverse action letter out of the file cabinet at work. It had been sent to another employee for something they'd done or not done on the job. I typed it word for word addressing it to Buck Wilson. I signed the superintendent's name on it and mailed it to Buck. Buck checked the mail before I got home and read the letter. He immediately called me and read the letter to me. He was so upset that he was shaking and almost unable to speak. I could hardly stop myself from laughing over the phone. Buck would do anything I suggested to save his job. The two or three times I tricked him, I always suggested that he call his psychiatrist, Dr. Langford, to see if he would admit him to the hospital to dry out. I usually had to make the call because he felt I could talk the doctor into anything. Now I know that was his way to get me do the work. He wanted me to ask the doctor for help for him instead taking responsibility for his own illness.

As usual, Dr. Langford admitted Buck to the Washington Hospital Center. There he had to make up his bed, participate in group therapy and eat all of his meals with other alcoholics and drug addicts. He felt he didn't belong there. In his mind, he was better than the other people there. In the long run, the program did not work for Buck. I believe that he was admitted 10 different times. His pattern was to stop drinking for a while, return to work, get involved with another woman, get caught, start drinking, beat my ass, drink for three or four months, receive the letter from the job that I had mailed, and then go back to the hospital to dry out again. This was a never-ending cycle. At the time, I didn't realize that I was just as sick as he was for enabling him and playing all those crazy games while trying to get him to sober up.

CHAPTER 26
We Conquered the Problem

As far as prostituting was concerned, God and I had conquered my problem. I had not been over to Aunt Claire's house for at least three years. The Creator and I did the work. I thank Him today for turning my life around. My life could have continued down the same road of self abuse and misery.

I decided within my heart that I was going to be a true Christian and wanted to be baptized. I went back to my home church, which had a new pastor. Rev. Beale told me he had his secretary to look up my record and found that I had been baptized when I was six months old and didn't need to be baptized again. I knew this was true, but I had an inner need to recommit myself to my Creator. I felt a renewal of my life and my spirit and felt the need to have my sins washed away.

Since Rev. Beale wouldn't re-baptize me, on the advice of Mama M, I visited different churches until I found one that I liked. I started going to the First Seventh Day Adventist Church. I was impressed because the members took their bibles to church and actually studied them. The women wore no make-up; they were naturally beautiful. Most of the worshippers were slender and most of them were vegetarian. They were warm spirited and welcomed me with open arms. I attended the church for approximately one year and asked if I could be baptized. The pastor was happy to oblige, and on September 25, 1975, I was baptized as a Seventh Day Adventist.

My godmother, Zepora and her family, and Mama M were all present at my baptism. We had a celebration that day with a special Sabbath dinner at Mama M's house. I learned a lot from the members of the church and from the writings of Ellen G. White, one of the founders of the Adventist Church. I ended up studying the religion so much that years later, I researched myself right out of the church.

CHAPTER 27
My Mother's Affair

In the meantime, my parents were still going to parties and fighting. My mother met a guy by the name of Alfonso Beane. Not only did Alfonso drink, he smoked marijuana. He and my mother dated for over seven years.

My stepfather suspected my mother was running around but had no proof. One night he became very angry, and my mother ended up with a broken leg. I happened to call the house right after the fight. My stepfather answered the phone, and I asked to speak to my mother as I usually did. He demanded that I come over to the house right away. I heard my mother screaming at him to tell me what he had done, and I knew she had been hurt.

I immediately called my brother and told him to meet me at the house. My brother arrived long before I did, and the ambulance and the police were already there. All I could hear my brother saying in a very firm voice was, "You know her age." My brother repeated the statement again, "You know her age." Apparently, my stepfather had told Andre that Mama came at him with a knife during the fight and he had to defend himself. My brother told his father, for the first time in his life, that if he found out that he was lying, he was coming back and was going to whip his natural ass.

Mama was admitted to the hospital, and we were told that her leg was broken in two places. My stepfather called his best friend, who was also his brother in the Masons, to go with him to the hospital for support. He told him, "Man I think I broke my old lady's leg." His best friend was Alfonso Beane. Alfonso played it real cool. He acted like a buddy and he asked my stepfather, "Why in the world would you want to beat on your wife?" My stepfather had no idea that his best friend Alfonso was doing it to his wife.

In the end, my mother told my brother that she tried to use a knife on my stepfather. She lied because she did not want father and son fighting. She stayed in the hospital two weeks. Alfonso visited her when my stepfather was at work.

When my mother came home, I begged her to stay on the first floor of the house where there was a small powder room near the kitchen that she could use. The living room had a sofa bed that had never been used. I also reminded her of how she liked to talk on the phone to Alfonso and her many friends, and I was afraid she would get caught. My stepfather had a way of coming back home and sneaking through the side door into the basement and listening to our conversations from the basement extension. For years he'd been listening to my mother's conversations without anyone knowing that he was in the house.

When my mother was well enough to go visiting, she asked me one Saturday morning if I would take her downtown to P Street where Alfonso rented a furnished room for their trysts. They had been meeting there for years. Against my better judgment, I took her there around 11:00 a.m. I decided to visit with them for a while and I sang while Alfonso played his guitar. Then, I went home and cleaned my apartment and cooked dinner. I went back to pick Mama up around 6:00 p.m.

When we arrived back at my mother's house, her brother Jimmy and Grace and Jim Albertson were waiting to see her. Grace and Jim Albertson were two of my mother's school friends. Uncle Jimmy said that he had heard about the fight and wanted to see how his sister was doing. My stepfather sat around giving my mother and me strange looks. I knew he was wondering where we had been for so long. Shortly after arriving there and after speaking to everyone, I left because I had a husband to go home to.

The following Monday morning, my mother called me at work from the third floor of her house. She told me she had just talked to Alfonso, and he said that he had enjoyed my company on Saturday. He also said he appreciated that I brought her to visit him. We laughed about how bad he played the guitar and how bad my singing had become since I left the church choir. We both said goodbye and hung up. Approximately 30 minutes later, I answered my phone at work again and it was my stepfather. He said, "Hello Ms. Stevens. I mean Wilson. Tell me how long your mother and Alfonso have been going together." My heart fell all the way down to the floor. I started shaking because I knew just what had happened. I said, "What are you talking about?" I could hear my mother saying, "Stop your lying." That was her way of letting me know he really didn't know anything. My mother could be so naïve at times. I told him in a very calm voice that even if I knew anything, I would never tell him. He hung the phone up. I called back and didn't get an answer. I was so afraid he would kill her that I called the police. They told me they could go to the house, but if they didn't get an answer, there was nothing they could do.

My mother finally called me around 2:30 p.m. and told me that my stepfather had taken her to Alfonso's job to confront him. He asked Alfonso how long he and she had been seeing each other, and he told Alfonso that my mother had confessed. Of course, my mother told Alfonso that he was lying. To make things worse my stepfather called Alfonso's house and told his wife what he thought. Alfonso ended up threatening his wife and telling her not to talk to my stepfather again. He also confronted Matthew with a gun and told him to stop calling his house and talking to his wife. Times were different back then. People were bold and got away with doing crazy things.

My mother stayed with her husband until another big fight occurred right after her leg healed. In a jealous rage, he took the keys to her cab and would not let her have them. He also threatened to shoot both of her knee caps off, and he kept her a prisoner in her own home. She couldn't even go to work. My mother ended up finding her keys and leaving while he was at work. She stayed with me until she found her own apartment. She left my stepfather sometime in 1976, just before my brother announced he was getting married. My mother and Alfonso continued to see each other until 1984.

CHAPTER 28
Growing Apart

Life went on and I continued in my new-found religion. I learned lots of good things and made lots of personal changes, but my husband was still the same person. We didn't have as many fights, but we still had them. I ended up catching Buck with another woman and confronted him about it. He reacted by starting to beat me again, but this time I pulled a gun on him. I wanted to shoot him but couldn't pull the trigger. He ran over to me, took the gun away, and punched me in my nose so hard that I thought it was broken. A day later I had a black eye and I couldn't touch my nose. For about the twentieth time, I thought about leaving him, but I didn't.

I didn't find out that my nose had actually been broken until 1998 when I had an asthma attack and needed an x-ray of my sinuses. That's when the doctor told me my nose had been broken and had healed wrong. I began to laugh and she asked me, "What's so funny?" It all came back to me, and when I explained to the doctor how my nose had been broken over twenty years earlier, she couldn't see the humor in it.

In the fall of 1976, at the age of 25, I went to the corporation counsel's office to take out a restraining order. Buck and I had had another fight and this time I was pretty banged up. I had had enough. I think he knew it too. He kept asking me the night of the fight if I was going to the corporation counsel's office the next day. I insisted that I was not going, but after I got up and took a shower, I headed directly there. I called my office from a pay phone on the way and stated that I was not coming in that day. I asked them to tell Buck that I was at the doctor's office, if he called. I knew that he would find that believable. I also called my friend Margaret Malone and asked if she would let me rent a room from her.

When I arrived at the corporation counsel's office, I met one of the many law school interns working there. This particular man was a short, white guy with blond hair. He was kind of cute and very young. He took my information and told me he would send a letter requesting Buck to appear for a consultation. Two weeks later, the letter arrived requesting that the two of us come to the office for a meeting.

When the intern asked Buck if he had hit me, he answered that he hit me only because I had caught him cheating. The intern then told Buck that he was working on a case where another complaint was filed by someone else who worked for the jail. They claimed that Buck and some other guys had beaten them the same way that I described being beaten in my complaint. He read Buck's statement from the interrogatory, which said that he had never hit any of those men. He stated, "Yet your wife is here complaining how you beat her in the same manner." The intern then informed Buck that if he ever heard of me complaining again about being beaten by him, he would see to it that he spend time in jail. I never had to worry about Buck ever hitting me again. Later on, I found out that my father had gone to Buck and threatened to kill him if he ever laid a hand on me again. After that, I said and did just about whatever I wanted to.

By the beginning of 1977, I got tired of Buck's running around. I guess I finally started believing that I deserved better. Maybe that was God working in my life. I knew it was time to leave, but I wasn't sure how to go about it. During that time, Buck received an invitation to his son's graduation. Buck had always denied that the young man was his son even though he had been married to the boy's mother, Cora. He also denied that he had ever been married, but they had two children and they all had the same last name. I asked Buck if he wanted to go to the graduation. His reply was "Let sleeping dogs lie."

Once again, I caught Buck cheating. This time, I just told him I was tired and would be leaving. He got drunk as usual, but this time I didn't complain, nor did I type the usual letter. I just let him drink until he couldn't see straight. I told him I thought it would be best if he had someone close to him to help him out during his times of need. He didn't understand what I meant. So, I called his first wife and told her that I felt that Buck needed to see his children and that they needed to see him. They needed to bond and get to know each other. I felt Buck would grow old and lonely all because he was a stubborn alcoholic who thought everyone had abused him. I agreed to get him dried out if his ex-wife would allow the children to come from Kentucky for a visit. She informed me that she didn't allow her children to go anywhere without her, so I agreed to pay for all three of them to come and stay with us in our one-bedroom apartment. How stupid could I have been?

Buck went into the hospital again, dried out, and went back to work for two weeks. Cora and the children arrived three weeks later. The children didn't look like Buck, but who was I to question it? When they arrived, we unloaded the car, and my mother and I took the kids sightseeing because I was very anxious for Buck and Cora to talk. They did more than talk. He was drunk before we got back home with the kids. I could tell what happened when I walked into the apartment. The guilt had gotten to Buck and he had started drinking again.

Cora and her daughter Dee Dee slept in our bed while I slept on the floor in the same room. Buck and his son slept on the pull-out sofa in the living room. I got up early and sat on the sofa beside Buck. We started talking about our sightseeing tour with the children. I noticed that he really wasn't paying that much attention to me, but when Cora got up to go to the bathroom, he got up and walked over to her and kissed her right on the lips. They acted as if I wasn't even in the room.

When Cora finished in the bathroom, I asked Buck to join me in the shower because I needed to talk to him. He insisted that he wanted to stay and entertain Cora. I told him that she could entertain herself, but I needed to clear something up. Once we were in the shower, I told him I knew what went down and as long as I was living in that apartment with the name of Wilson he was going to respect me. I said that I wouldn't be there very long so he didn't have to worry about me being a Wilson much longer. He never said a word. Then I got out of the shower, got dressed and went to the kitchen and told Cora I was sorry that she came with her children. I told her she, too, needed to respect my home and me. She never said a word.

Cora and the children ended up leaving a day earlier than planned. I had not paid her for the tickets, but I gave her a check and stopped payment on it the very next day. She was not going to fuck my husband in my house and get away with it. I was not surprised at all that had happened. I didn't blame them. I blamed myself for allowing Cora and the children to stay with us for those few days. I should have put them in a hotel, but I had some misguided idea that I was helping Buck find some sense of family with his children. I had already made up my mind to leave, but it still hurt that he and Cora carried on their affair right in my own home.

Two months later, Buck helped me pack my boxes, not out of the goodness of his heart, but because he was probably somewhat concerned that I would take things he didn't want me to have. Before leaving, I told him that I was going to give him six months to stop drinking and sleeping with other women. It was strange that he would choose this time to confess his unfaithfulness, but he ended up telling me about several of his affairs, including the time he accused me of giving him a venereal disease. As we continued to pack, he admitted that he had actually been infected with gonorrhea by a female employee who worked with us. He told me that he blamed me, but he had actually forgotten the last time he had intercourse with me because of his drinking. At that point, all the anger over his behavior had left me. I was totally numb.

In reality, the whole time I was married, I was in and out of different doctors' offices. I had a nervous stomach for which the doctors prescribed Librium and Valium. They said that my stomach was tied into knots from all the stress I was under. At that time the stress came from my husband and all of his problems. I also had to repeatedly see a gynecologist for vaginal problems. I was in the doctor's office every three weeks with a different complaint. After I left Buck, the infections went away. I only go for regular checkups now. That alone is enough proof to me that Buck was passing infections to me from the different women he slept with. Yes, I was a prostitute and I'm sure I got infected that way also, but Aunt Claire always had us see her doctor for a regular shot of penicillin to keep the infections away.

CHAPTER 29
Starting Over

My mother had been living in a studio apartment, and when I told her I was leaving Buck, she convinced me to share an apartment with her. She said that I wouldn't be able to afford a car note if I had no one to help with the rent. I think she honestly believed that I couldn't take care of myself and she had me believing it too. That kind of thinking was hard for me to overcome.

On August 27, 1977, I moved into a two-bedroom apartment with my mother. I moved all of my things to the new apartment that day and was unpacked and settled by 3:00 p.m. I think I surprised everyone who knew me when I was finally able to leave Buck and stand on my own two feet. The day I left, he was drunk and had been drunk for over two months. He had stopped caring about his job and his bills. He wasn't even concerned about the car accident he'd had where he did a considerable amount of damage to the other person's car. I kept worrying about him and wondering if I should let him stay in that apartment knowing he was not taking care of himself. I was sure he'd be crawling around on all fours. He was a diabetic with no cooked food to eat. My concern for him prompted me to check on him, so I went to his apartment and found him passed out cold on the floor. When I shook him awake, he acted as though he didn't know who I was. He eventually recognized me when I said that I had come back for more of my things. Then he started ranting and vowed to kill me if I took anything else.

Buck admitted he needed help this time, and although I felt that I was not obligated to help him anymore, I called Dr. Langford and scheduled an appointment. I took Buck to his appointment at the end of the day during rush hour traffic. It was against my better judgment, but I did it anyway. When Dr. Langford asked Buck what was wrong, he said he was upset because his wife was leaving. Dr. Langford knew that I was leaving because we had talked about it in one of our individual sessions. The doctor had convinced me that Buck was using me as a crutch.

Buck and Dr. Langford agreed that he needed to go to the hospital for a quick dry-out period, and I agreed to take him home to pack his clothes and then take him to the Washington Hospital Center by 7:00 p.m. After I got him packed, he wanted to go to McDonalds for a Big Mac and french fries and then to the liquor store for a half pint of J & B scotch. He sat in the car and ate the food in the hospital parking lot until 7:15 p.m., hoping that his bed would be taken if he was not checked in by 7:00. But once he was admitted and settled in his room, I gave him a kiss on the cheek and said goodbye. He never once asked me to stay or to come back, and I never offered.

About a week later, Buck called me and asked me to pick him up from the hospital because he had been discharged. I took him home and got him settled. He expected me to clean the apartment, but all I did was change the bed linen so he could go to sleep. He was very upset, but in my heart I knew he needed to start taking responsibility for his own actions. He tried to tell me that I had left him at the worst time of his life, but I knew that any time would be the worst time. He had hit rock bottom, and it was time for him to climb back up.

While all of this was going on in my life, I was still visiting my father. I told him that Buck and I were separated, and that I needed to make some decisions about my future. My father was glad I had left Buck, but he was not happy to hear that I had moved in with my mother. He said he could not visit me as long as my mother and I were living together. I told him that I could not pay a car note and rent too. He didn't offer me a solution, so I did what I felt I had to do.

As he promised, he would not visit me, but I went to visit him and Zelma regularly. During that time, I began to have problems with my father, and I felt that it was the beginning of the end of what I thought was a beautiful relationship. He had withdrawn from me emotionally.

My visits to my father's house became less frequent because I could sense that he was uncomfortable when he was around me. I always took gifts for him and Zelma whenever I visited them. He eventually told me to stop buying them gifts and to save my money. However, I continued to take them and he never refused them. They always thought my gifts were so beautiful. For Valentine's Day that year, I gave him a framed picture of myself, which he placed on his dresser. I also gave him a beautiful 100 percent cotton navy blue and white robe for Father's Day.

Zelma called me one day and asked if I could meet her for lunch. I met her on a Thursday at Health's A Poppin, a very health conscious deli. She knew that I liked that particular sandwich shop, and it was around the corner from her job. When I arrived she gave me a hug and told me to order whatever I wanted. I ordered a chicken salad sandwich with a soda. It was a beautiful day. The sun was shining brightly and there were no clouds in the sky for miles.

Zelma told me that my father was a very honest man and that when he gives his word he doesn't go back on it. She told me that, when they got married, he told her that I had been born, but he didn't have to worry about me ever coming into their lives because my mother had told the courts I was not his child. She said he went back on his word when he allowed me to come into their lives. Then she told me that when she met him in 1952, he was still crying over my mother. He was actually crying himself to sleep at night. She also told me that my mother was having an affair with my stepfather while she was still living with my father. I asked her why she was talking to mc about my mother in that manner. I could see the anger in her face as she went on to say that my mother was no good. I told her she could only go by what my father had been telling her for years and that she didn't know my mother and she should know better than to talk about a black person's mother like that. I said that I was angry and I would be speaking to my father about this conversation. I never finished my sandwich.

I called my father at work and asked to see him alone. He insisted that I come out to the house on Sunday morning, and I could hardly wait to get to the bottom of the situation. I arrived around 10:00 a.m., and we all went into the living room. I should have known that he and Zelma had discussed this in great detail before we met for lunch that day. I remembered later on that it was their pattern to plan these meetings together.

My father started the conversation by telling me that my mother and I had no class and that my mother was a horrible person. He said he had caught her and my stepfather in their bed in Chapel Oaks. He also said that my mother wasn't decent enough to call him and tell him that he was my father. I tried to argue that a child is not responsible for what their parents do, and therefore, I had no control over what my mother did or didn't do. I also said that she was not there to defend herself, and I felt it was unfair of them to take their frustrations out on me. I didn't say it, but I knew that my mother had her own side of the story to tell.

My father told me that I was greedy and was just like my mother. When I asked what he meant, he reminded me that I had asked if he would leave his father's watch to me. He came in possession of the watch when his father died, and when he showed it to me, I remember asking rather nonchalantly if he was going to pass it on to me. It was a beautiful watch, but it wasn't valuable. I only wanted it because it was something that belonged to my grandfather. He was someone I had not had a chance to bond with before he died.

The conversation ended when I started to cry. My father and I walked outside together, and I asked him not to change his will on my account because I felt it would upset Zelma, and I wanted to show him that I was not a greedy person. I didn't understand how he could call me greedy. When he didn't respond, I asked him what was really wrong. We'd had seven years together, and I couldn't understand how he could end the relationship like this. He replied that he had tried to feel something for me as a father, but he couldn't, and he flatly said that he could not be my father. He said that my stepfather had raised me, and in my own words, I was more loyal to Matthew than to him. I explained that my feelings had changed after seven years and that he had unreasonable expectations that I could be able to call him daddy and feel an instant bond after being apart from him for so many years. He and I had to learn to love one another first.

I found myself begging my father not to end the relationship, but he was very firm. He said, "I have no feelings for you as a father." I remember his final words to me. "You are no longer a member of the Wren family." Then he told me to take care of myself and to lose some weight. I left his house in tears. Once again, I was rejected and abandoned by my father. His actions reinforced in my mind that I was never really loved by anyone and that I was an unlovable person. I drove away shaking, and almost totally blinded by my tears.

Not knowing what to do, I went to Norman's house and told him what had happened. Norman was an old friend who'd been my knight on the white horse when my parents were fighting. He worked for the Metropolitan Police Department and he and his white partner often intervened in my parents' fights. Norman said that I hadn't had Lawrence

Wren in my life for all these years, and I didn't need him now. He went on to say that he thought Matthew Stevens, Sr. was my true father. I left Norman's house crying even harder. No one understood how I felt. Inside I was an emotional wreck and felt completely rejected, like I had been thrown away by my father.

I went home and didn't say anything to my mother for a day or so. She knew something was wrong because she kept asking me why my eyes were so red. I ended up calling my godmother to tell her what had happened. She told me, "You must have done something to make this man turn against you the way he did." I tried to explain my side of things, and she just kept saying the same thing over and over again.

After two or three days of crying, I finally told my mother everything that happened at Daddy's house. She immediately told me she thought I must have asked him for some money or something. Everyone I talked to said it must have been my fault. No one tried to see things from my perspective, and no one had any words of comfort. I called my grandmother on my father's side, Aunt Della, and Aunt Etta. They all told me to pray and let the Lord handle it. My cousin Charlene told me, in so many words, to forget about him and Zelma. She said they were not worth my tears. My heart was broken, and I couldn't let go. I hurt more than I did over the breakup of my marriage and any other relationship that I'd lost. I was devastated.

After crying for days, I decided to tell my father the story the way my mother had told it to me years ago. This is when the anger started to surface. I wrote him a letter and my best friend Mava delivered it to his office. I started off by telling him that one of his closest friends told me that he was getting ready to leave Zelma for a white woman when he met me. I also told him he was lucky to have a child because my mother had told me he could not have children when they first married. She told me that my father had contacted some kind of disease and needed a doctor's help in order to get her pregnant. I was very angry and lashed out. I said some things that could not be taken back. He never responded to my letter and that only made things worse for me. I found myself suffering from depression and tried everything I could to come out of it. I prayed and tried to keep busy but my mind wouldn't allow me to let go.

I believe two years passed before I saw my father again. His stepmother died and Charlene called me and asked if I would come to the funeral. She said she was not going to tell anyone that I was coming. I arrived in Charlottesville three days later, and I stayed with Charlene until it was time for the funeral. When we arrived at the house, my father greeted me with a kiss and a big hug, just like nothing had ever happened. My aunts were glad to see me, especially my aunt Etta from New York. When it was time to go to the church, the funeral director called out the names of those who would ride in the family car. He called everyone's name except mine. I was shocked. I had to ride in the last car all by myself. I started to cry because I felt my father was being cruel. Then something inside of me said, "Don't cry. You have this nice car all to yourself."

After the funeral, the pastor shook my hand and said, "I'm sorry for your loss Ms. Wren." That was all I needed to know that I was a true Wren. It was confirmation for me that I looked just like my father, and people could tell I was part of the family. That eased the pain for a day or so. After that, I ended up burying it in the back of my mind where I thought it would never surface again. I didn't know that it would later come back with a vengeance.

The years following the funeral went by fast. I look back and really can't remember much of what was going on during that time in my life. I truly believe I was just going through the motions. I remember weighing 168 pounds around the time my father banished me from his life. Two years later I weighed 224 pounds. I know I was using food to cover up my feelings.

CHAPTER 30
Moving On

In the fall of 1979, I started dating Troy Martin, a married man. Troy was from Sunderland, Maryland and worked in D.C. We would meet at a hotel on Saturdays and sometimes during the week. Later he asked for a key to my apartment, and I gave it to him. For some reason he would think that I was having an affair with another man if he called and there was music playing in the background.

I felt bad about dating a married man, but Troy had me believing that his wife was on her deathbed and I would be the next Mrs. Martin. We dated until 1983, when I moved to Calvert County. Someone told his wife that I was dating her husband and was moving to the county. Troy tried to deny the affair until he became concerned that his wife was dating someone in her church. He begged me to call her and straighten things out, and I did. I called her and took responsibility for everything. I never told her that her husband had told me that she was on her deathbed and would be dying from cancer at any minute.

After that incident, I vowed that I would never date another married man. I lost a lot of respect for Troy after knowing that he had been dating me for five years and only stopped because he thought his wife was dating someone too. When he thought he was going to lose his wife, he became suicidal.

Late in 1979, I left D.C. government and started working for the federal government. My new employer allowed me to take certain classes to improve performance or to qualify for other careers. I became very interested in the law and decided to start taking some paralegal classes, which I enjoyed very much. I finished all of my required courses, but I became disillusioned by the lack of protection the law provided for black people. I repeatedly saw court cases where justice was served mostly for people who did not have my skin color.

In 1981, I moved into a one-bedroom apartment. I enjoyed living alone. My mother was upset with me over the move, but I had to prove to her that I could take care of myself. She would tell people that I didn't pay my half of the rent or that I came back before the month ended and borrowed all the money back. I will admit there were times when I borrowed money from her, but never more than $20.00 or $30.00.

At one point, I worked as a secretary for another federal agency. I met two wonderful people who were always able to find the good in everyone. Their names were Mike and Reyna, and they continue to be good friends of mine to this day. Mike was the supervisor and Reyna was one of the attorneys. Mike always thanked me every Friday for a good week of hard work. He saw talent in me that I was not aware of. He appreciated my ability to organize and make things happen. He encouraged me to apply for an upward mobility position in space, property and telecommunications. The change in position would be a big career improvement.

The Friday before the application was due, Mike was reading over my qualification statements to make sure they were correct and acceptable. The next thing I knew, there was a bomb threat, and I rushed to Mike's office and told him that we had to vacate the building. For some reason he didn't believe me. He thought I was afraid of completing the application and accused me of trying to get out of making the copies. I was terrified, but I started laughing so hard I almost urinated on myself. Of course, I left the building immediately. I tried to wait around outside for Mike and the rest of the staff, but I never saw them in the mass confusion of people. When my ride came, I went home.

The next day Mike called me at home and asked where my application was. When I replied that it was on my dresser, he told me to get it to personnel by 7:00 a.m. Monday so that I would still be in the running for the position. I did as he told me, still hoping that someone else would get the job, but as it turned out, I was selected, and I stayed with that agency as a space planner and telecommunications specialist for eight years.

CHAPTER 31
Exploring My Identity

I have never been a good reader. I had trouble learning to read because I never really knew how to sound out the words correctly. To compound the problem, I always had a problem with my sight. Later in life, after I developed a hunger for reading, I practiced by taking the necessary time to sound out the words. I tried hard to pronounce them correctly, and I even looked up the meanings of words I didn't understand. Today I still have a problem with some words, but I know I have improved almost 100 percent compared to my reading ability in the seventies and early eighties.

Back then, I went through a phase when it was important for me to claim my heritage and discover more about my roots. I began reading many spiritual books, as well as political books on white supremacy and the movement to suppress black people from rising up in the world. This phase of my life was an important step in my personal healing journey. My beliefs later evolved from that point, and I no longer believe as strongly about those issues. I now believe that people of all races are affected by those in positions of power in the world. We all need to learn to find our voice and educate ourselves on our personal human rights. We need to claim our power. I think those most affected are those of a low socio-economic background due to their lack of access to education and appropriate healthcare.

I read almost all of the books by Sister Ellen G. White of the Seventh Day Adventist Church. I learned a lot, but I also had the feeling that something was not right with what I was being taught. I felt that the church was holding something back from its flock. I decided it was important for me to have a better understanding of church doctrine, and I began researching it when a friend brought me a tape from a Sabbath service by Elder Jacob Justice. On this tape, Elder Justice made certain predictions and stated that black people were worrying about a time of trouble before the time of trouble could get here. He stated that we had a lot more to be worried about than just the time of trouble. He said we should read books like *The Spook Who Sat By the Door* and *The Choice*. We needed to know what was happening right in our own back yards. He said that the government was experimenting with cows, sheep, and other animals, and that they would soon be experimenting with us in the same way. He also stated that we would be in a moneyless and cashless society, and the country's leaders would say it was because of the war on crime. And he said that the United States was in the process of changing the dollar bill to have a metal thread running through it to make it harder for counterfeiters to duplicate it. I believe that most of the things he spoke of have come true.

I still have a taped speech by Elder Justice, wherein he said that we need to know our history so that we could see the future. The first book I read after I heard him speak was *The Choice* by Samuel Yette. It empowered me and helped me gain a stronger sense of myself. It set me free. Then I read *God, The Bible and The Blackman's Destiny* by Rev. Barashango. Those books had me look at Jesus Christ as a black man and not as the blond haired man with blue eyes I had been exposed to in the past. Since reading those books, my beliefs have evolved to recognize that Jesus is a spirit and his color is love.

The books started me to think about the holidays we celebrate and the food we eat. I learned a lot about how commercialism affects all people in the world. I felt a major transformation deep in my soul from my new outlook and the truth that I had begun to experience.

I read on my lunch hour, or as soon as I got home in the evening, and I would spend all day Saturday and Sunday reading. I read books by numerous authors who enriched my life and helped me grow as a person. Other books that impacted my life were *Before The Mayflower*, *They Came Before Columbus*, and *Fire In My Bones*. All the while, I was listening to WPFW Radio Station, which broadcasted a lot of information through speeches of Malcohm X, Minister Louis Farrakhan, Martin Luther King, Jr., Ivan Van Sertima, Charles Finch and others like Huey Newton, who had been with the Black Panthers back in the sixties. I used to sit at my desk all day and get energized from knowing that we had such great leaders and such knowledgeable individuals who were willing to share the information, and most of all, take a stand against white supremacy. These individuals were not afraid of telling us the truth. On Sunday mornings,

I would never miss Listervelt Middleton's show, "For The People." He interviewed historians like Dr. John Henric Clark, Dr. Na'im Akbar, and my all-time favorite Dr. Frances Cress Welsing. I learned more then than when I was in school and the hunger for more and more information kept me up until 1:00 and 2:00 a.m. How I got up on time to go to work, I will never know.

I had asked the Creator to allow me to read only truth, and my prayer was answered right away. I never thought to pray for acceptance of the truth that I had read or was reading. I walked around for months looking like I had stuck my finger in an electrical socket. People would come up to me and ask, "What is wrong with you?" My answer would always start off with, "You know I read this book," but I could not fully explain what I had read. After two years or so, I realized that I had to quit reading for a while because I was getting sick mentally. I constantly worried about things that were out of my control. Finally, I prayed and asked that I be able to accept what I would be reading and the things I had read in the past. My prayers were answered again, and I found that I could have intelligent conversations about everything I had learned.

One life changing truth I learned through reading is that we need to be self-sufficient, meaning in part that we need to grow our own gardens because the American food supply has become more and more saturated with chemicals and hormones. After reading that disturbing information, I felt that my mother and I needed to move back to Calvert County where we would have enough property and resources for a garden. I agreed to share the house with her and support her since her Social Security checks were pretty small. I moved on December 27, 1982, and my mother joined me on January 1, 1983. The house was small and filled with mice and all kinds of animals I had never seen, but with a lot of hard work and a couple of renovations, we converted it into a comfortable home.

Shortly after relocating, I joined Nick Short's vanpool to get back and forth to work. I rode in the vanpool from 1984 until May of 1990. I was the only black person in the six-passenger van. I remember that some of the riders would ask me questions from time to time, and they sometimes seemed surprised when I answered them intelligently. They even came right out and said, "You are smart," which I interpreted to mean, "You're smart for a black person."

CHAPTER 32
When Phillip Died

My best friend and mentor, Mama M., died in September 1988. She loved the Lord and didn't mind sharing His word with you. I could call or visit her at any time and she was always glad to see me. She greeted me with a hug and a kiss on all of my visits and teased me about my weight. I would say, "Mama do you think I've lost any weight?" She would always say, "Turn around and let me see your hips." Then she'd say, "No you don't look like you've lost any this time." When I was depressed, she always had comforting words, and I knew anything I shared with her would stay between us. She would take my problem to the Lord through prayer and direct me to do the same. Sure enough, I would see change. I even learned about the herbal kingdom and vegetarianism from Mama M. She was in my life for over 35 years, and I still think of her often. Reflecting on her words makes me feel better about any situation I am struggling with. She was my champion. Every child and adult need someone who cares for them unconditionally. Mama M was that person for me.

Phillip, my oldest brother, came home to live with us because he was ill. We didn't know how ill he was, but by August 4, 1988, we found out he had cancer of the liver. My mother took very good care of him until his death on October 8, 1988. I really didn't cry very much when Phillip died. I knew he was no longer in pain, and I also knew he was in a better place.

When Phillip was alive, he liked to live on the D.C. streets because he wanted to drink and have a good time. He never wanted to live in a house where he had to pay rent, especially when he found out he could live in the shelters.

I broke down and cried when we requested a military funeral for my brother, and the officials said they could not get the honor guards to the church on time. They had another service before ours. I took the phone from my mother and told those people that my brother had served this country, as many of our men have, and they had better get to the service on time. I felt that he got neither the medical care he was entitled to, nor the treament he needed for alcohol addiction. We sat and listened to the choir singing those sad old funeral songs until the honor guard got there. They arrived 20 minutes late.

Once Phillip was buried and all the thank you cards were sent out, I felt a sudden release and relief to know he was in a better place. I no longer worried about him being in the shelters, nor did I need to worry about someone taking advantage of such a sweet, yet troubled soul.

CHAPTER 33
Meeting Elliott Wade

On a Wednesday in October of 1989, my clock radio came on at 4:15 a.m. with Roy Hamilton singing "Ebb Tide." The programmer was Elliott Wade, also known as The Love Source. I called in to tell him how nice it was to wake up to such beautiful music, and he asked me if there was any particular song I wanted to hear. I asked him to play anything by Dinah Washington or to continue playing something by Roy Hamilton. Every week, I would wake up and listen to the Love Source's show, and I would call from time to time to let him know what a wonderful job he was doing.

The programmers for the station are volunteers and don't get paid for their hard work or dedication. Back then they had to use their own records, tapes, and CDs. One day, I sent Elliott a tape of some of Roy Hamilton's less known music that I thought he might like. Sure enough, he had not heard the two albums I sent him, and he commented that they were so scratched he could hardly hear the lyrics.

One morning, Elliott asked me if I wanted to dedicate a song to my loved one, and I told him that I didn't have anyone at the time. To my surprise, he announced on the show that he had spoken to a Tommie Wren who needed someone special in her life. I was so embarrassed that I called him right back and asked him to never mention my name again on the air.

In January of 1990, I told Elliott that I would not be listening to his show for a while because I was going to have surgery and would not be up at 4:00 a.m. When he asked why I was having surgery, I told him about the accident I'd been involved in that caused me to need neck surgery, and how I was a little afraid of having it done because of the risks involved. He then asked me if he could have my telephone number to check on me during my recuperation. I gave it to him never thinking he would call, but after my surgery, my mother came to the hospital one day and said, "Some man named Elliott called and wanted to know how you are doing." She said that she was tired of talking to him because he was calling every evening to check on me. I had not had anyone pay that kind of attention to me in a long time.

When I arrived home, Elliott called me every other day to see how I was progressing, and I thanked him for being so concerned. We had developed a telephone relationship and during the four months I stayed home to recover, he would send me his taped shows in the mail. I liked most of the music, but a lot of it was straight ahead jazz, and I just didn't appreciate that type of music. Sometimes, he would send me additional tapes that he made just for me. One in particular was "Make Me a Present of You" by Dinah Washington. By then, he knew that I loved Dinah Washington's music. Along with the tape, he sent a picture of himself.

Everyone who knew about my telephone relationship with Elliott said that he was probably wondering what I looked like. Afterall, he had sent a picture of himself to me. So I sent him a picture of a horse. He did not like the joke. Deep down, I was not comfortable with my appearance, but I later sent him a picture of me with two other women, and didn't tell him which one was me. He ended up calling to ask me to identify myself in the picture. He gave me his home telephone number, and I immediately asked him if he had a wife, because I had vowed to never again get myself tied up with a married man. He assured me that he was not married.

Sometime in August of 1990, he called me at work and said he would like to deliver a tape to me at my job. I had invited him to my home on several occasions but he would always tell me that he was too busy to visit. I agreed to meet him within an hour. I was nervous because I had gained weight and was having a bad hair day. I should have told him, "No, let's do it another day," but I didn't.

He was not what I expected. He wasn't even someone I would take a second look at as boyfriend material. He was kind though, and he had a pleasant smile and a beautiful personality. I thought that we could be telephone buddies.

We continued to call each other from time to time, and we would meet for breakfast on the Wednesdays he worked. I invited him to my home again, and he finally showed up for breakfast on January 18, 1991. After breakfast, he looked over my record collection and was somewhat impressed. He told me that he felt I was not romantically interested in him, and I told him that I really had not thought about it. We continued our friendship and met for breakfast or lunch, whenever time permitted.

On April 16, 1991, Elliott invited me to come to his home for dinner. Neither of us had any intention of building a lasting relationship, but that night, our relationship went to a new level. He was interested in sex and I was desperate for it also because I had been without it for a very long time. Before we slept together, he tried to tell me that he had a friend he was seeing from time to time, but I interrupted him and said that I was not going to be with a man if I knew he was involved with someone. That was a big mistake because he decided not to tell me about his other relationships.

After that evening, we did not go our separate ways. For over seven years, we continued to see each other every weekend and sometimes during the week. He began to introduce me to several of his male friends, but he never introduced me to their wives. I asked him if I could attend a jazz concert with him once, and he replied that he would never take me to the same places he had taken his friend. I began to question him about this friend because I was feeling restricted. We didn't go to many public places and I wasn't allowed to go to his place unless we planned it in advance. I could not just show up; I had to be invited.

When Elliott finally got around to telling me about his friend, he told me it was an on and off relationship and it had been that way for many years. For a long time, I accepted what he said. Only when I decided to give him a surprise birthday party in 1995, did I truly find out that he had been lying to me. His friends, Chester Cunningham and Nobel Green, tried to tell me what was going on, but I had tunnel vision where Elliott was concerned. I had gotten most of the names and addresses of his friends from Chester, Nobel, and George Lynch, and I found the other addresses in the telephone directory. His friends seemed to want the party as much as I did, so they added names to the growing list of people. They knew the low down, but they thought it was funny that he was involved with two women and were eager for some drama. Finally, Nobel and Chester asked me to meet them for lunch. I didn't know what to think. I had never met them for lunch before because I thought those old men were going to try something inappropriate with me, or tell Elliott some lie. Having been raised the way I was, all kinds of things made me paranoid. I didn't want to have someone tell Elliott I was trying to date any of his friends. Finally, I spoke with them separately over the phone, and they each told me, in their own way, that Elliott had a "main squeeze." They said that if I had the birthday party, everyone would wonder where she was and who I was. They also told me that Elliott had a temper and if I tried to give him a surprise party, he might not react well. They were afraid he would surprise me and show a side of himself that would not be pretty. They said that they would feel better if I let him know about it in advance. They would help me in any way I needed with the party, but I had to get his blessings first.

I took their advice and told Elliott on a Tuesday evening after work. After I finished telling him the story, he hung up on me and didn't speak to me for a week. When he finally called, he got upset with me for wanting to do something nice for him. He eventually agreed to have the party, but he wanted to pick the people who could attend. That was control with a capital "C," but that was okay with me.

I wrote out the invitations and put them on my desk to be mailed closer to the date, but a co-worker mailed them without asking me because she assumed they were ready to go out. Consequently, everyone got their invitation about two months before the party. When Elliott found out that the invitations were mailed, he hit the ceiling. He told me to call everyone and cancel the party. I got so angry and embarrassed that I told him to do it himself. Again, he did not speak to me for a week.

By this time, I was ready to let the relationship go. I knew he had not been honest with me, and I always wondered where this other woman was. He was with me most of the time, so I did not understand when he would ever have time to see another woman. If I called his house and felt something was not right, I never mentioned it to him. If the shoe had been on the other foot, Elliott would have been upset with me. I had to be at home by the phone when he called or I was questioned.

In the mid-nineties, I started reading more books on African culture. A couple of my friends were taking a class called "The Awake Lecture Series." I took it in 1995, and it was worth every dime I paid. It changed my life completely. I learned so much about myself and my people that was not written in the text books in the schools that I attended, and I started to feel a kinship to African people all over the world. I also started looking at my body as the Temple of God. Although I am still overweight, I am now more selective about what I put in my body. Changing bad habits takes time and discipline when you have made unhealthy choices all your life.

In the late nineties, I was in a carpool with Harry Kirkpatrick and Darryl Jones. Darryl looked white, but talked, walked, and even joked like a black man. He only dated black women on welfare, or prostitutes. I sensed that he was in deep trouble, and asked him if he needed someone to confide in. I let him know that I would be willing to listen. One day he broke down, and told me about his drug addiction, and how he was beaten up every now and then by the women he dated because he didn't always pay them their money. I would laugh to myself and tease Darryl about his irresponsible behavior at his age. I believe he was 62 years old, and he seriously needed to straighten up his life. When I told Elliott about Darryl's problems, he told me to stop riding Darryl in my car. He was worried that I would get hurt by the people he was mixed up with. I was somewhat afraid myself, but I had faith that the Creator was always with me for my protection.

One day Darryl called me from work and asked for a ride home. He had not ridden with me that morning, so I was surprised when he called. I told him to meet me in front of my car, which was parked on the side of the building where I worked. When I arrived at my car, he was leaning on it with a suitcase in one hand and a suit on a hanger slung over his other shoulder. Little did I know that Elliott had come to my building to see me because he was on his way to the Pennsylvania Jazz Concert and would not see me for a couple of days. We'd had some words about why I couldn't go with him, and he wanted to smooth things over. He was surprised when he saw Darryl standing by my car. He assumed I was taking another man home since he was going to be out of town.

I didn't know Elliott had seen Darryl leaning against my car. When I got home I called him as usual but his attitude was funky. I asked him what was going on because I had a feeling he was taking his other woman, Theresa, to the concert. I had reason to believe that they were back together.

I thought Elliott was upset about our fight, and I started questioning him about where our relationship was going. I also wanted to know about his relationship with Theresa. What a time to ask that question. He was upset and very defensive. He told me that Theresa and he had a very strong relationship. He also said he didn't know where I got the impression that they had an on and off relationship. He said that those were my words, not his. I was so hurt.

Elliott then explained that he came down to my job to surprise me, but he left because a man was leaning on my car. I was so upset that I was having a hard time understanding what he was talking about. Then I remembered that Darryl rode home with me and I called Elliott later that evening to tell him who the man was. I started laughing because I thought it was pure craziness. My laughing only made him angrier, and then he really went off. Ranting like a jealous boyfriend, he told me that I had no business driving that man around in my car. He couldn't believe that I had disobeyed him and continued to give Darryl rides to and from work. The way he acted only made me laugh harder.

After Elliott calmed down, his tone was different, but he was not able to take back what he said. In spite of my fits of laughter, his words cut deep into my heart. Deep down, I knew that I would never be his "main squeeze."

The next morning, I picked Darryl up and we had a good laugh when I told him what happened. I also told him that I would not be able to pick him up anymore. I let him know that I was afraid something might happen because of his drug dealings. I reminded him of the time he had been beaten right outside his building by some men he owed money for drugs. Darryl didn't like it, but I had to take care of myself.

Elliott and I stopped talking for a month or so, and then he called me just to see how I was doing. When he was feeling guilty, he would play special songs for me to have me think that he still cared. We continued to see each other until he became seriously ill and could not walk. He was confined to his bed from June 1998 until May 1999.

I'm not exactly sure when Theresa became aware of me. Maybe it was when I sent Elliott a dozen roses when he was hospitalized in 1998. He called me every day to tell me how beautiful they were and he said everyone, including the hospital staff, talked about them. I knew then that Theresa was probably upset. Elliott acted as if he didn't care if he hurt her feelings or not. I began to tell him to show his appreciation for what she was doing for him. He expected her to wait on him hand and foot, and when I told him that he was using her, he admitted it was true.

I stopped visiting Elliott on a regular basis when I discovered he had given Theresa a key to his place. I didn't think it was right for her to do all the work and then have to deal with me as the other woman. He was on a special diet and was losing weight. I would give in every now and then and take him a meal. He would ask me to bring him a cheeseburger from Wendy's or pancakes from the International House of Pancakes. We ate together and I would make sure I left after an hour. On my way out, Elliott would demand that I take all the trash with me so that Theresa wouldn't know that anyone had been there.

On occasion, Elliott would ask me to come and give him a bath since he was unable to get around well enough to bathe himself. This was his way of asking for sex. When I insisted that I was very uncomfortable in his house knowing that Theresa had a key, he would tell me she was not allowed there unless she called first to say she was coming. I told him I felt he was still using her. He never answered me.

I started talking to Elliott about becoming more spiritual, which was a foreign concept to him. The more spiritual I became, the harder it was to accept being treated disrespectfully by any man. It was also hard to accept how he was treating the other women in his life. I got tired of hiding my presence in the house and decided to cut the strings between us.

CHAPTER 34
Family Crisis

In December 1997, I bought a condo in College Park, Maryland. It was so nice living by myself again. I needed and enjoyed the quiet times. I had just finished reading *Of Water and of Spirit* by Malidoma Patrice Some. The book was about a young man who was kidnapped at a very early age from his homeland in Africa and was taken to a Jesuit mission school. There he was harshly indoctrinated into the European ways of thought and worship. The writer shared a touching description of his natural and supernatural experiences, and I knew in my heart that he was not lying. After reading his book, I felt a need to experience a tribal ritual for myself. It reminded me of my need to be baptized. I also decided it was time to take another class, but I wasn't sure what I wanted to study. I just knew I was searching for something more.

Malidoma Some's wife, Sobonfu E. Some, wrote a book called *The Spirit of Intimacy,* wherein she states that everyone is connected, and describes that connectedness to every living thing in the universe. Her book gave me a deeper understanding of everyone as a spirit. It also made me consider the need to respect every living thing on Earth. I even developed a new respect for little insects that I never liked before.

On September 29, 1998, I had another experience with family dysfunction, but this time it involved my niece, Cindy. We were notified that Cindy was in a coma at Prince George's Hospital and was in the intensive care ward. No one on the hospital staff could tell us why she was in a coma. The only thing we knew was that she had a seizure at work, and had been rushed to the hospital where they initially thought that she had a brain tumor. I got the feeling that the doctors were treating her like she was a drug addict. Eventually, one of her doctors told me that they found drugs in her blood work. I did not believe Cindy had been on any drugs except for the ones prescribed by her family doctor. One of her doctors told me that you can get any drug you want on the street, even those prescribed by a doctor.

We were very worried because they gave us no hope about my niece's recovery. Although I was not very close to Cindy, I did not want to see the child of my oldest brother die. I called my friend Terry Tipton, who is a medical intuitive and asked her if she would visit Cindy to find out whether her spirit wanted to leave. If she was ready to die, I was going to let her know that it was all right to let go. Terry visited my niece and said that half of her wanted to stay and the other half wanted to leave. I believed that she longed to be with her mother and father who both passed away from cancer in 1988. So, I felt it was okay to tell my niece it was all right to let go and let the Creator take her with Him if that is where she wanted to be.

The doctors wanted one spokesperson from the family to make decisions about Cindy's medical concerns. She had numerous friends coming to visit and they wanted one person to be responsible for her welfare. Since I lived closer to the hospital than my 79-year-old mother, I became the spokesperson. I also looked for an attorney in Protective Services of Prince Georges County to become the guardian for her meager assets. That was a hard task, but I handled it with numerous calls back and forth to the hospital and Protective Services. I also had to make several calls to the rental agency for her apartment, to the bank for her car loan, and to her cell phone company. No one would accept my story that Cindy was in a coma and could not speak or pay her bills. I also had to remove her furniture and clothing from her apartment so that it would not be put on the street once she was evicted.

Several of my friends advised me not to go into Cindy's apartment by myself. When I asked them why, they said that they believed that she was possessed. I didn't understand what they meant until I visited her one day. I started talking to her to try and bring her out of the coma. When I told her that I would be moving her possessions from her apartment to a storage facility, she suddenly tightened her body, sat up, opened her eyes, and growled at me. I immediately thought of the movie the "Exorcist," and of course, I got out of there fast. A nurse saw me hugging the wall outside Cindy's room and asked me if she could help me. I replied, "Cindy did something that really frightened me," and she said "You know, Cindy is not all here." I had no idea what she was trying to tell me.

That evening, I made several telephone calls to different people to ask for help. One of my friends stopped by, and when I told her of my experience that day, she told me to ask Spirit to give me the information I needed. I did just that, and two hours later, I began to get incredible information from people who knew nothing at all about Cindy's problem. My hypnotherapy instructor called and said that people who do drugs and hangout in dark places, draw negative energy to themselves. The next person to call was Cindy's friend from Baltimore, Wallace. He told me that he was concerned because Cindy was not her normal self. When I asked him what he meant, he said that when he visited her, "She seemed as if she was possessed." Oh, the power of prayer.

Around 10:00 p.m., Cindy's pastor called and asked me how she was doing. I told her that I was not sure because she had done something that had frightened me. She asked, "What did she do? Tell me sista because I already know what she did. It was the devil. I heard her the other day, but I dismissed it." I was reluctant to repeat the story because I believed that Christian ministers were not responsive to possession stories, although the Bible speaks of them. Desperate for help, I told her the story, and she agreed to take two of her prayer warriors to the hospital with her to pray for Cindy. She told me to ask the doctors if they would allow her and the other two people 15 minutes with her. The next day, I told the doctor that her pastor wanted to have a prayer session for 30 minutes, without interruption. He looked me straight in my eyes as if he knew exactly what was going to happen, and said, "I don't care what they do as long as they don't give her anything."

I waited until Tuesday of the following week to visit Cindy because I was afraid to go back. Before entering her room, I said a prayer of protection and braced myself. What I saw next was my fully grown niece babbling like a little baby. I immediately called her pastor to see if she had been to the hospital to pray, and to let her know what was happening. She confirmed that she'd held the prayer session and everything was fine. Within a week and a half, Cindy regained her ability to speak and started talking like an adult. She came out of her coma on October 31, 1998. My stepfather died the next day.

My brother, his wife Gloria, and my stepfather's wife Jenny, helped me plan the funeral. Most of the responsibility for the arrangements fell on me because my brother and his wife had no experience in those matters, and Jenny was simply unable to do much of anything.

CHAPTER 35
My Nervous Breakdown

The emotional pressure from my stepfather's death, issues on my job, and the responsibility of taking care of Cindy caused me to have a nervous breakdown two weeks after the funeral. I had read that the death of an abuser has a powerful impact on the victim, and found this to be true. I cried and cried and cried until I had no more tears left. I couldn't control my thoughts or get any rest for days on end. Finally, my medical doctor and my psychiatrist placed me on bed rest for three months.

I returned to work on January 25, 1999, and found that the work was too much for me to handle. I left again March 30, 1999, almost in the same shape I was in on the day of my breakdown. I was no longer able to handle the normal day-to-day stress of working.

I decided to move back to Calvert County in December 1999. At that time, I was still talking to Elliott and trying to keep some kind of friendly relationship with him, but it had become too difficult. One day, he called and asked me to come to his house and manage his accounts for him. He also expected me to give him a bath and play with little David—the name he gave his penis. I refused; I had no intentions of doing what he had requested of me. He called me again and became more demanding. I put him off and waited until he was not home to leave this message on his answering machine: "What is the highest good for all concerned in this matter?" I repeated it three times, then I told him that it was not my responsibility to pay his bills, or to bathe him, and it certainly was not my responsibility or desire to play with little David.

I have been seeing Dr. Welsing since my nervous breakdown, and she determined that I have Post Traumatic Stress Disorder (PTSD). The PTSD resulted from the culmination of my life experiences of abuse and stress. Up until that point, I had developed sufficient coping skills to live a relatively peaceful life, but the government job was the final straw. My mind could no longer compensate under the extreme pressure placed on me at work.

As my therapy continued, I waited for a decision from the Equal Employment Opportunity Commission on my complaint against my agency. I filed the complaint because I believed that the managers on my job set me up for failure by placing expectations on me above and beyond my job description. I believed in my heart that they decided that I was doing too well, and stacked the work so high that I would never finish it. They knew that I was overwhelmed with the responsibilities they were piling up on me.

I lost my EEO complaint after paying two attorneys over $16,000 to represent me. However, the Office of Personnel Management finally approved my disability retirement, after denying it three times. Upon review of my case, an attorney for the Merit Systems Protection Board said that I should not have been denied the first time.

CHAPTER 36
The Party

On November 18th 2000, I celebrated my 50th birthday with a party at the Washington Navy Yard. I invited 75 people, but only 55 showed up. Zepora and her family came, and Pamela March was there. I had known them since childhood. Though they were several years older, they always spent time with me and looked out for me when I was a child.

Everyone looked great. My brother and his family came, and were all dressed up. Even Cindy was there, fully recuperated from her illness. I had taken special care with my hair, makeup, and my outfit. I looked fabulous, and I was in a festive mood when the party began. Tina Campbell was my emcee. My brother was in charge of the music and video taping, but, for some reason, he didn't do the taping. After what happened later on, I'm glad that there's no tape to remind me of my humiliation.

For some reason my mother had a negative attitude about the party. She didn't want to wear the appropriate attire, and she refused to sit at the head table. In fact, she refused to cooperate with anything I asked her to do.

The roasting and toasting began with Mike, who had a lot of positive things to say about me. Next, Aunt Joy stood to introduce herself and let everyone know that she was there to support me. Then, my mother stood up and told everyone that I was bossy. "Bossy, bossy, bossy," she kept repeating like I ran a slave factory or something. I couldn't believe that my own mother couldn't say one good thing about me. Her roasting of me left me more than well done.

My mother's pastor, who was invited only to please her, told the group how she used to stop by the house and eat and nap whenever she wanted to, before I moved back home. It was clear that it was a critical statement, though some would have thought that she was teasing.

My brother's roast was equally as annoying to me. He said "we do not get along" three times during his short speech. I thought to myself,

"What in the hell is going on with these people?" By that time, I was near tears. I always thought family members were supposed to keep their dirty laundry hidden. I don't know what I would have done if some of my friends and other family members had not saved the day by asking, "Who are you talking about?", and saying that they never knew me to be bossy, just direct and helpful.

When it was my time to speak, I got up with a smile and thanked everyone for coming to celebrate my birthday with me. As a joke, I said, "Yes, I am somewhat bossy, but I was my mother's mother in a past life, and she somehow forgot that small detail." Somehow, I managed to make it to the end of the party without bursting into tears.

Needless to say, I talked to my mother about her little speech and she didn't think it was so bad. It was her opinion that everyone knew what type of person I was. A few days later, my mother and I were arguing and I realized that she was angry about something else. She finally told me that I had made her pay for installation of a new well on our lot, instead of letting her buy a car. I had to remind her that I had given her $3,000 towards the well, which cost $4,900.

At that point, I knew I had to get away for a while so that I could cool off. I stayed with my friend Joan until I could get an appointment with my psychiatrist. My emotional health was in such bad shape that Dr. Welsing had me admitted to the Psychiatric Institute of Washington on November 22, 2000, the day after my birthday. It was Thanksgiving time, but I didn't want to have anything to do with my family, and I didn't feel like I had anything to be thankful for. They had really upset me by ruining my birthday party. I felt that I had thrown away the $2,000.00 that I spent on the party.

CHAPTER 37
Struggling Emotionally

In January 2001, Elliott had a heart attack and was kept at Veterans Hospital for two weeks. His doctors required that someone be with him at all times after his discharge. He asked me to move in, and I agreed to stay for a week to give him enough time to find a nurse to take care of him. Well, all hell broke loose because Theresa and his new girlfriend, Linda, found out that I was there and hit the roof. Theresa refused to come see him while I was there. I can understand how they felt, but what they didn't know was that the relationship, at that point, was nothing more than a friendship. I stayed with him out of the goodness of my heart.

On February 12, 2001, I had gastric-bypass surgery to help me lose weight. Elliott told me he would come see me in the hospital and hold my hand; instead he went to a jazz concert, and I didn't hear from him until after I had been discharged two days later. His actions told me that he didn't care for me at all. I let him know exactly what I thought of our friendship, and I refused to go anywhere near his house afterwards.

My surgery was a success. By October 2002, I had lost over 63 pounds, but as I lost weight, I looked more and more like my father. At times, I could not look at myself in the mirror because my resemblance to him reminded me of our estrangement and made me remember over and over again that he had rejected me—again. I had to work hard in therapy to control my feelings over how I looked. I even bought wigs to try and change my appearance. Considering how far I had come with the weight lost, one would think that I'd be ecstatic, but I was depressed, lonely and afraid.

Elliott was admitted to the hospital several times after we broke up, and on August 15, 2006, he died from chronic heart problems. He is missed by his family, friends, and fans, and in spite of our rocky relationship, I miss him too.

CHAPTER 38
Trying Again with My Father

When I was 52 years old, I reunited with my father after writing to him in November of 2002 about his sister's funeral. I wanted to know why he had not come to the services for Aunt Etta, his last sister. Along with the letter, I sent a copy of my memoirs and told him it was up to him to contact me. I wanted him to know how I lived and struggled most of my life when he was not there to help me. I knew that he was all alone because Zelma, his wife of over 40 years, had died in October 2001. I was my father's only remaining blood relative.

My father called me one week before Thanksgiving and asked me to visit him. When I arrived, he greeted me with open arms. We had Thanksgiving dinner together, and it was the best Thanksgiving ever for me. I had so longed for a good relationship with him. I truly wanted him to know me as the wonderful person I had become. Since it was so obvious that he was severely depressed, I moved in with him to help him out. He would sleep all day while I cleaned the house and cooked his favorite foods. We played cards when he was well enough, and talked about his past. I learned a lot about him and I cherished every minute we spent together.

Unfortunately, he was not able to forgive the things of the past and neither could I. He couldn't forgive my mother for leaving him, and I couldn't forgive him for not being a father to me. I thought that, if he truly loved me, he would have rescued me from the horrible childhood I experienced.

My father was still trying to control me emotionally. He said that he thought I should move in and stay with him on a permanent basis. I told him I had a responsibility to my mother, too. He didn't like what I said, but he seemed to accept it. He would go into a rage every now and then about how my mother cheated on him. I listened and tried to be understanding, but it was frustrating to listen to him. From a cultural perspective, it is unacceptable to talk negatively about a black person's mother. All black people know that. I eventually started defending my mother because of my loyalty to her.

I tried to convince my mother to apologize to my father so that he could move on with his life. Eventually she agreed and asked me to bring him to our house. She said she wanted the relationship between us to blossom, but I know that a part of her still didn't want to share me with him.

Sometime around March of 2003, I took him to see her. She gave him a hug when she greeted him, but he was uncomfortable and acted like a little boy who really didn't like hugs from women. I took him on a tour of the house and told him how small it was when we initially moved in. He was very impressed with my house and all of the renovations we had made. He was also impressed with my antique furniture and accessories. I inherited my love of antiques from him.

He and my mother finally sat down to talk. I left the room so that they could have some privacy. The meeting didn't last long and wasn't very effective. Apparently, my mother reminded him of the time he came home professing his love for another woman. She said that was when she decided to have an affair and leave him for my stepfather. She apologized for her actions with hopes that he would apologize for his. He accepted her apology but refused to offer one to her.

Back at his house, my father said that he had changed his will and named me as his beneficiary. He said more than once, "I have taken you as my daughter and I'm giving you all this." I took this as a sign that he was still questioning my paternity.

Daddy asked me from time to time how my uncles and aunts Sally and Joy were doing. I told him that it was time that he saw them and others that he had not seen in a long time. I asked if he would come to Easter dinner so that he could reconnect with some of the people from his past. He didn't want to go back to my mother's house, but he reluctantly agreed to go after I convinced him that some of the guests wouldn't be able to travel all the way to his house.

The dinner was lovely. Daddy had a chance to visit with several people he had not seen for over 40 years. I also invited my brother and his family because my father wanted to meet them. They all enjoyed themselves. Daddy appeared a little stressed in the beginning, but as time passed he seemed to have a good time.

The next day Daddy let me know that he thought I did a great job pulling everything together. It meant a lot to him to be able to see my aunts and uncles. The last time he had seen Aunt Sally was when I was a baby. She gave him a picture of me that was taken the same day he had visited her to see me when I was six months old. He looked like he wanted to cry.

Upon meeting my father, my brother could easily see how much I resembled him. That was the confirmation that his father was not my biological father. Likewise, Daddy was able to see the striking resemblance of my brother to my stepfather—the man who'd stolen his wife. They were both noticeably uncomfortable with each other.

After the dinner party, my father kept calling and asking me to stay with him for a while. When I went back, he kept complaining about how I spoiled my brother's children. He said that they didn't appreciate me. I knew that he was jealous and upset because my brother didn't talk to him very much. At that point, I decided that it was time I had a life of my own because I was spending most of my time helping my parents, and they didn't appreciate my devotion to them.

CHAPTER 39
I Am My Father's Child

My father and I got into another argument about my mother. I told him again that what happened before my birth was not my concern. Then he made that statement again, "I have taken you as my daughter and I'm leaving you all this." Well, I demanded that we have DNA testing to clear his mind. He did everything he could to convince me not to take the test. He went to see Dr. Welsing to try to convince her to stop me, and he also tried to get his therapist to talk to me. When none of that worked, he had one of his friends to talk to me. Each of them told him that I was entitled to know the truth. I desperately wanted the test to prove to him once and forever that I was his child. I made the appointment for the testing sometime in August 2003.

A couple of days before the test, he told me that he wanted us to have lunch, kiss and never see each other again. In his words, "We weren't getting along and would probably never get along." But in spite of all he tried to do to stop it, the test was done at last. Within four weeks, the results came back confirming by 99.9 percent that he is indeed my father.

He was so happy. He called me the minute he got the results and asked if we could celebrate. I agreed and he made reservations for a Sunday dinner at Mrs. Kay's Toll House in Silver Spring, Maryland. He told me how he used to take the senators and congressmen there in the 1950's when he was a chauffer, and how he had to wait in the car while they ate. We also talked about how happy he was about the test results and how nervous he had been about the outcome. I told him I always knew the results would be positive. I was overjoyed on that day of celebration. I had no clue that my joy would end.

My father remarried in 2006 and decided to end our relationship again. To this day, I don't understand why. I know that I was a good daughter to him and my mother, but I am powerless to change the way he thinks and acts. I have moved on with my life and found ways to fill the void. Regardless of how he treats me, I am my father's child and I love him.

CHAPTER 40
Meeting Stanley

In January 2003, after posting a personal ad, I met Stanley Warren. He was a very honest, sincere, and kindhearted man. He loved to talk about white supremacy and its affect on us as a whole. It was a topic I was very interested in before I began to grow spiritually. Although I had changed some of my views on the topic, something about him made me listen. It had been so long since I'd had a stimulating conversation with a man that I just listened to everything he had to say. We talked until the early hours of the morning.

Our first date was at a local Red Lobster Restaurant. I enjoyed his company and found him to be attractive. My biggest concern was that I would end up being his caregiver if we developed a relationship because he was confined to a wheel chair. After our date, we talked and I made it very clear that I didn't want to be a caregiver because I had been playing the role of a nursemaid all of my life. I also told him that I was taking care of my mother and had tried to reunite with my father, and that I needed to continue to work on that relationship. I still had hopes that my father would come to his senses. Stanley seemed to understand. He had four children and seemed to be a very committed father. I really admired his devotion to his children.

It was important that we develop a strong friendship before taking the relationship to a sexual level. After some time, we felt a certain closeness to each other and began sleeping together.

I told Stanley about my past because I was writing my memoirs, and I wanted him to hear it from me before he read about my life in a book. I really let my walls down and told him everything, including my secret life as a child prostitute because it was important to know if he would still accept me once he knew everything. He was shocked, but seemed to be understanding. Eventually, I shared the manuscript of my book with him.

Stanley helped me to see my life and my family in a different way. He showed me that my family did not know how to love me the way a family member should be loved. Even today, I often feel as though my family takes me for granted. Sometimes it seems like they're there for me only if I'm giving them something.

Stanley wanted me to take some college classes because he felt that I needed to be doing something with my life. So I decided to enroll in a real estate class at Prince Georges Community College to please him. After all, he and all of his children had earned degrees. They often made me feel like I was lacking education. Based on some of their actions, I now feel like they were lacking common sense.

I truly thought that I had fallen in love with Stanley, although he was not as affectionate as I would have liked him to be. There was always an emotional distance with him. His mother had died when he was 20 months old, and he missed out on a lot of the affection and nurturing he would have gotten from her. I found myself trying to change him by showing him love and affection the best way I knew how, but he was uncomfortable with the attention I gave him, and he did not understand my need for it. He said he had not been affectionate in his marriage either. He decided to use the information I shared with him about my childhood to prove his point. He said he didn't understand my thinking since I had been taught by my parents that it was okay to hit, hug, and kiss, all in the same day. That was the first time I knew that I should have kept my mouth shut about my childhood. His statement was very painful. Stanley won. I was no longer comfortable being affectionate with him and my love for him slowly died because of his words and his actions.

On October 20, 2003, I had a tummy tuck, which was the second part of my by-pass surgery. My stay in the hospital was supposed to be only 23 hours, but it turned into ten days because my kidneys failed while I was on the operating table. Something happened during the surgery to cause them to shut down, but no one would tell me what. I was too sick to ask questions anyway. I relied on Stanley a lot during that time. He was there every day asking the right questions and keeping me company even when I didn't know he was there.

Just prior to having the surgery, I had become depressed again because my family life was growing increasingly painful. My father and I had not spoken since Father's Day, and my brother and I had had an argument. For some reason, he was directing some misplaced anger towards me. He always seemed to be angry at me, and I had no clue why. After putting up with his attitude for way too long, I told him he could no longer talk to me in the nasty tone he used in our last conversation. That day, I hung up on him for the first time in my life.

My mother and I were not getting along either because she was so critical of my relationship with Stanley. She was threatened by the attention I gave him because she feared that he would ask me to marry him and I would leave her.

I was so depressed that I asked the Creator to take me home. I was tired of fighting and trying to make people understand my feelings. I was also tired of feeling guilty for mistakes I had made in my life, like the prostitution and the abortions, and I no longer wanted to feel unloved and unworthy of love. I prayed just before they put me under and asked God to take me. I wanted to be happy and thought that the only place I could be happy was heaven.

At one point during my stay in the hospital, my room became very still and dark. The doctor hadn't come by that day, but he had been in the day before and said that I needed to be put on a kidney dialysis machine. They had already prepared my body for the procedure. I was so devastated that I called for my spirit guides and the spirits of my grandmother and Mama M to come and sit with me. I felt their presence with me and it was comforting. Sometime during that day, I felt myself drifting upward and then I saw a bright light in the distance above me, but no one was there to greet me. I shouted as loud as I could, "Where are you? I thought some one is supposed to come and greet me. You all lied!" Then something said, "Be quiet. Look straight ahead." I looked up towards the light, and there appeared an outline of a person. I couldn't make out who it was, but I knew someone was there. It was very beautiful and a little frightening. Sometime right after I saw the person in the light, I woke up and thought I had been dreaming. I found out later that I'd had a near death experience.

I forgot about the incident until Stanley came to visit, and I told him about it. Much later, I read a book on near death experiences, and I connected it to what happened to me. Since that time, I have decided to do whatever I can to help those who need to be comforted and consoled. I have always felt that that is my purpose in life, and I feel even stronger in that belief today. The experience helped me to discover my life's calling.

My father came to see me in the hospital and he brought his girlfriend (the woman he later married) with him. She looked so much like his dead wife, I almost called her Zelma. His birthday was October 29th, which was the day I was discharged from the hospital and I called to wish him a happy birthday. Two or three days passed before I called him again and got the shock of my life. He was so upset that I hadn't called him sooner that he told me to never call him again. I was still holding the phone with my mouth wide open in shock when he hung up. That was the final straw for me. I vowed never to let him or anyone else hurt me that way again. I never wanted to have a hardened heart, but I prayed that my heart be protected from people like him.

Stanley took good care of me at his house once I was discharged from the hospital. He changed my bandages everyday and cooked for me. My mother was having a fit because she wanted me home with her. One day I had Stanley take me home, and I showed her my incisions. When I asked if she felt capable of taking care of them, the look on her face told me she couldn't. My mother has never been the nurse type, and the few days I stayed with her convinced me even more that she could not adequately handle the bandaging.

After I left Stanley's house, I ended up going to my doctor's office to get the bandages changed. One day, one of the nurses called my primary care doctor into the examination room to take a look at one of my incisions. It was infected, and I was lucky that she could see me so quickly. It was not funny then, but I can look back on it now and laugh at how many times I had to go to my doctor and have her clean and bandage me. She was so wonderful, and she never charged me for my visits.

I have often wondered why Stanley and I got together in the first place. Spirit had us meet for a reason. I still care about him but I don't think that I could have stayed in love with him in the long run. Although he had issues of his own, he was more comfortable playing therapist to me.

One day Stanley asked me to marry him, and all kinds of triggers came up for me. I knew in my heart I loved him more than any man I had ever been involved with, but I started questioning whether I could remain true to him. I questioned whether I would end up like my mother, having affairs and lying about them. I even wondered if I would end up taking advantage of him or being abusive to him because he was in a wheelchair. It all boiled down to my fear of commitment and my fear of becoming a permanent caretaker. Also, I really never thought Stanley loved me enough to stand up to his children on my behalf. I didn't feel secure with him, and I also worried about his ability to take care of me since he was disabled. We broke up sometime around September 2004.

I know now that when the right man comes along I will be faithful, loving, and compassionate. Those past feelings were just fears that are no longer with me.

CHAPTER 41
What I've learned

Initially, I decided to put my story in a book to help me through the healing process. Now, I hope that my experiences will help others see that you can recover from trauma. I also hope that it will help others see how abuse can destroy a person. It has a ripple affect on the lives of the victim and everyone they care about.

I've learned a lot in the past year. I found out that PTSD does not always occur after one incident. It can be caused by a number of events during one's lifetime. When I first learned the symptoms, I realized that I could have been diagnosed a long time ago, even when I was a child. However, the symptoms often remain dormant until stress causes them to surface.

Some children and adults have a hard time expressing their feelings and asking for what they need. I remember feeling that no one, especially my mother, understood what I was trying to say when I was a child. She used to tell me that I was making things up. I truly believe that she couldn't or didn't want to deal with my issues, so she brushed them off. I had no choice but to develop coping mechanisms to protect myself from dangerous and excessively stressful situations. I started to sense when things were going to happen because I knew what the energy felt like. I had been experiencing crisis my whole life.

I now realize that my intuition is very tuned in to things that would be upsetting to me. I believe that that is God's way of preparing me to deal with whatever happens. I have learned that God will give me what I need to avoid a crisis or to get through one, as long as I ask for His help. I continue to go to therapy for treatment of PTSD, and I continue to work on my core issues, as well as those caused by my job.

I am still in therapy working on the issues of childhood abuse, sexual abuse, abandonment, and mental cruelty. I have written a couple of letters to my abusers and I am at peace with my parents and how they treated me. I am learning to love and accept myself and do the things that make me happy. I know I have a beautiful heart, and I respect everyone's soul.

Through the years, I have had to find positive people outside of my family and made them my family. Some of these individuals have treated me better than my own blood relatives.

It is February 10, 2007, and I am feeling wonderful about life. I have truly forgiven my father, my stepfather, my mother, my aunt, and Harold Jones. I am happier today than I've ever been. I must say, I love my mother more today than yesterday, because I now know that she was terrorized by my stepfather and was afraid to try to protect me. She too was a victim.

I'm not in a romantic relationship and haven't been in one since 2004, but I'm enjoying life and exploring my calling. I graduated from the All Faiths Seminary International in 2005 and became an Interfaith Minister. I am a volunteer hospital and hospice chaplain at a Maryland hospital, and I also volunteer at another local hospital as a victim's advocate. When a victim comes in for a rape exam, I stand next to her and hold her hand to help her through her ordeal. It's nice to be able to offer her support and wisdom and to let her know that the worst is over and that she is no longer a victim; she is now a survivor.

I have started a foundation, Spiritual Connections, Inc., to help women and children recover from sexual abuse. I plan to conduct private and group sessions with women and teenagers for healing and support, and I intend to continue to share my experience of overcoming difficult relationships and abuse. Victims of abuse find many ways of continuing the cycle of abuse by hurting themselves. It's important for me to do what I can to break that cycle and create awareness about the many options there are for healing and recovery.

For me, it was important to be willing to do whatever it took to heal. A big part of my healing journey was my spiritual growth. Once I accepted God in my life, I began the process of breaking self-destructive and self-abusive behavior patterns. My first step was making a commitment to my Creator that I would do whatever it took to heal. Even though I have reached a place of peace today, I see it as my personal responsibility to continue to work on myself in whatever way I can. Most of the work I do today is through metaphysical healing modalities.

I have worked with a psychiatrist, a therapist, a medical intuitive, and other healing professionals. I saw Terry Tipton of Far Cry Farm twice a week for over two months during my darkest hours right after my diagnosis of PTSD. Terry directed me to drink lots of pure water and raw vegetable juices and to eat light vegetarian meals. She also had me do a detox cleanse to clean the toxins from my body, and she gave me supplements to help repair my nerves and immune system. It was necessary to physically restore my body to help me process all the emotional issues I was releasing.

After working with Terry, I worked with a shaman to experience soul retrieval. A shaman is able to look at your heart and soul and tell you what karmic issues you brought here with you this lifetime. He or she helps people reconnect with parts of themselves that they have disassociated from due to trauma.

I've been a member of the Takoma Park Chapel under the leadership of Senior Minister Jim Webb for over eight years. Jim has prayed with me and for me. He and Terry have taught me to meditate and open up to spirit. I had to allow myself to get quiet and learn to listen to my own inner guidance and explore my connection with spirit guides and angels.

Another exercise I completed was an aquatic rebirthing. While partially submerged in water, I was actually able to visualize myself being born. For me, it was a rebirth into my new life. I was able to release pain and suffering that I had been hanging onto my whole life.

Like most women, I would like to be in a positive friendship and/or romantic relationship with the right man, but I find it very difficult to establish a meaningful relationship once my past becomes known. Our society has a tendency to blame the victim and not the abuser. It is very frustrating and painful to think that some men can't come to terms with the sexual abuse of a woman they might otherwise have a future with. The famous singer Billie Holiday, who was also a victim of childhood sexual abuse, summed up my feelings exactly in *I Never Told Anyone: Writings by Women Survivors of Child Sexual Abuse* by Ellen Bass, when she said:

> "It changed the way I looked at everything and everybody. There was one chance I couldn't take. I couldn't stand any man who didn't know about the things that had happened to me when I was a kid.

> And I was leery of any man who could throw those things back at me in a quarrel. I could take almost anything, but my God, not that. I didn't want anyone around who might ever hold this over me or even hint that on account of it he was a cut above me."

One day the Creator will send someone to me who will be able to accept me as I am and see the beautiful person I am inside and out.

While traveling on the road of healing, I have learned to choose wisely when choosing friends. I like being with positive people who are growing emotionally and spiritually. I do a lot of self-healing and self-help work to continue my own personal growth, and I try to let God direct me in all decisions and aspects of my life. I am no longer the plain brown Wren I used to be. I am reclaiming my power and becoming the bright spirit God intended me to be. I believe God has helped me on my healing journey so that I could follow my calling and help others overcome the trauma of abuse.

If my story has moved you to help victims of sexual abuse, please make a donation to my foundation. Donations may be made by Paypal, check or money order addressed to Spiritual Connections, Inc., P. O. Box 303, Owings, Maryland 20736. You may view my web-site at www.spiritualconnectionsinc.org.

Made in the USA